MICKY
FLANAGAN

Funny Geezer

MICKY FLANAGAN

ABI SMITH

JOHN BLAKE

Published by John Blake Publishing Ltd
3 Bramber Court, 2 Bramber Road
London W14 9PB, England

www.johnblakepublishing.co.uk

www.facebook.com/johnblakebooks 🅵
twitter.com/jblakebooks 🅃

First published in paperback in 2014

ISBN 978 1 78418 002 7

British Library Cataloguing-in-Publication Data:
A catalogue record for this book is available from the British Library

Designed by www.envydesign.co.uk

Printed in Great Britain by CPI Group (UK) Ltd, Croydon, CR0 4YY

3 5 7 9 10 8 6 4 2

Papers used by John Blake Publishing are natural, recyclable products
made from wood grown in sustainable forests. The manufacturing
processes conform to the environmental regulations of the country
of origin.

Every attempt has been made to contact the relevant copyright holders,
but some were unobtainable. We would be grateful if the appropriate
people could contact us.

To Lily and Henry

CONTENTS

ACKNOWLEDGEMENTS

Thanks to Toby and John at JB for making this possible – and for a subject that had me in fits of giggles from start to finish.

And a big thank you to all the usual suspects: Katharine for all your support, research, chocolate supplies and child-care duties. I can't believe how lucky I am to have found a friend like you.

To Granny and Grandman for always being there when I need you; same goes for my B and Toodle Pip.

And to Mr Smith for making me laugh on a daily basis for the past 15 years – even if you did forget to fill out the forms.

SOURCES

I have drawn on various newspaper articles as part of my research for this book. In particular the following newspapers, their supplements, magazines and news sources have been especially helpful: *Daily Mirror*, *Sunday Mirror*, *Daily Mail*, *Mail on Sunday*, *Daily Telegraph*, *Sunday Telegraph*, *Daily Express*, *Sunday Express*, *The Financial Times*, *Sunday People*, *Independent*, *Independent on Sunday*, *The Times*, *The Sunday Times*, *Guardian* and the Press Association.

The book *Learning To Labor: How Working Class Kids Get Working Class Jobs* by Paul Willis provided me with useful insight and background.

There have also been a number of blogs and websites that have been useful in the writing of this biography. These include:

www.mickyflanagan.com

www.contactmusic.co.uk
www.chortle.co.uk
www.facebook.com/mickyflanagan
www.bbc.co.uk/comedy
www.channel4.com
www.ticketmaster.co.uk
www.londonisfunny.com
www.alisonpeterspr.com
www.ckproductions.co.uk
www.comedycentral.co.uk
www.timeout.co.uk
www.comedy.co.uk
www.mailonline.co.uk
www.entertainment.ie
www.cix.co.uk
www.montessori.org
www.clickliverpool.com

In addition, Micky's appearances on TV and radio
and his live shows, such as The Out Out and Back in
the Game tours, have of course been a rich source of
information and anecdotes.

PROLOGUE

'Please welcome onto the stage, Mr Micky Flanagan!'

'My wife, she's very middle class. She loves to go out to a restaurant and say things like, "Isn't this lovely, doesn't it have a lovely ambience?" And I'll say: "I don't have a clue about..."'

The audience cackled with laughter. The dazzling spotlights were planted firmly on Micky, standing in the centre of the stage of the Brighton Dome on that warm summer's evening of 2009 but he could still make out the front two rows of the crowd and saw huge grins beaming back at him. He had everyone's attention and continued his now well-perfected, well-rehearsed 'red sauce' gag as everyone waited eagerly for the punchline. Apart from the comic pauses that allowed the audience to appreciate every rib-splitting line of the story – and for a confident

performer like Micky, sometimes saying nothing apart from raising an eyebrow to the audience is enough to heighten the gag even further – they didn't have long to wait to hear the climax of the joke.

'So, we're in this fancy French restaurant and something is ruining the ambience for me. There is no tomato sauce on the table. Setting up the very awkward situation where I've now got to ask for tomato sauce. I said to the waitress, "Excuse me, do you have any ketchup?" She went to the kitchen and I saw her coming back with a little pot. I stopped her, I said, "Don't go anywhere, love," and I took a sip of it. Then I looked at her and said, "Yes, I'll have a bottle, please."'

The laughter from the auditorium was deafening. Micky stood still and smiled back at them, chuckling to himself and pleased as punch with the reaction that he was getting. He knew he had struck a chord with the diverse members of the audience, revelling in the knowledge that few comedians enjoy such broad appeal, and feeling his fans' appreciation as their cheers reverberated around the space.

Micky left the stage in a buzz. The crowd loved him, and hopefully the thousands of viewers at home who were watching the last episode of *Michael McIntyre's Comedy Roadshow* loved him too. This is what he'd been waiting for. After 10 years of working every weekend in the pubs and clubs on the comedy circuit for a handful of people in a range of venues – some pretty grim, others worse

(the sort of places where you'd wipe your feet on the way out) – his dedication had paid off. People were clapping and cheering him because he was telling them about his life. And in that one gag, we get a whole lot of life story about Micky. Middle class versus working class; fancy restaurants verses red sauce. Words that have no meaning to an East Ender born and bred (what is an ambience?) but who is now living in middle-class suburbia.

From being too poor to afford Alphabetti Spaghetti when he was a youngster to dipping fancy bread in oil at his wife's dinner parties.

From drinking Stella Artoiris (Micky's pronunciation) to sipping from a nice bottle of Shiraz. If Micky had been called Eliza Doolittle, there would be some comparison – rising from the cockney working classes to earning a fortune entertaining the country.

A man-of-the-people in that he's admitted to stealing things in the past 'cos he believes certain foods are well over-priced (don't get him started on the price of motorway service station sandwiches!) and yet he can entertain the future King of England with his cheeky tales.

Micky to his fans, Michael to his mum, 'oi Flanagan!' to his mates… Micky's appeal is that you could see yourself having a pie and pint with him and staying on until closing time (you'd probably have a lock-in too, depending on the landlord) and yet he is a millionaire with 'more money than I know what to do with'.

But how had he become such a well-known, well-liked

character? From humble beginnings in the East End of London in the 1970s to selling out seven nights at one of the biggest arenas in the country, London's O2. From hating school as a youngster to going back to university in his thirties. From giving teachers grief as a teenager who got a detention every other day to standing in front of a class full of pupils as a trainee teacher, years later. Fish porter, window cleaner, painter and decorator, waiter in America... from doing 'f**k all' to entertaining thousands at more than 400 shows in two sell-out tours.

It's high time that we delve into the funny world of Mr Flanagan to discover more about his popularity, what inspires him and how he made the simple act of asking for ketchup in a restaurant a laugh-out-loud ordeal.

Chapter 1

EAST END WAY OF LIFE

'Michael... get yerself up the apples and pears
to Bedfordshire right now!'
COCKNEY DEFINITION: *APPLES AND PEARS*
(NOUN) STAIRS.

It was 1962, the year that saw The Beatles rejected by top record company Decca, while Cliff Richard was the golden boy of British pop and his hit single, 'The Young Ones', was topping the charts. It was the year that England lost to Brazil in the World Cup quarter-finals (Brazil went on to win the tournament), *Private Eye* was published for the first time and the BBC satire, *That Was the Week That Was*, first hit our TV screens. A pint of milk cost 1 shilling and 4d (equivalent to 6.5p now), a loaf of white bread would have set you back 11½d (4.5p), Harold Macmillan was Prime Minister and Hollywood sex

1

siren Marilyn Monroe was found dead in the bedroom of her Los Angeles home after an apparent overdose. Closer to home, the last trolley buses were taken out of service in London, the new Hyde Park underpass opened, while deaths from smog in the capital reached 60 for the year.

It was also the year that, on 7 October, Michael 'Micky' Flanagan first entered the world, born to Sylvie and Jim Flanagan in the London Hospital, Whitechapel.

The London Hospital, now called the The Royal London Hospital, is located on the south side of Whitechapel Road, Whitechapel, in the London Borough of Tower Hamlets. The 'Elephant Man' Joseph Carey Merrick spent the last few years of his life at the Royal London Hospital. For years Whitechapel itself was known as a very poor, working-class neighbourhood, probably still most famous as the area where London's most prolific serial killer, Jack the Ripper, reportedly killed 5 prostitutes in the late 1880s (there were 11 separate murders known to the police but it is widely accepted that 5 were the work of the Ripper).

As the youngest of 4 children, Micky was the second son of Sylvie and James 'Jim' Flanagan. Sylvie Smith, who was born in 1934 in Bethnal Green, married Jim in 1955, in Bermondsey, the same place Jim was born. Four years younger than James, she was twenty-one years old when she married him in a simple ceremony with close family and one year later, they had their first child, a daughter whom they called Patricia. Getting married young – or what is deemed to be young by today's standards – wasn't

unusual in the 1950s, it was a time when the average age for a woman to get married was 20. Sylvie was a machinist and Jim was a docker – a term used for someone who used to help load and unload ships in the Docklands area of London – who went on to be a welder and a Billingsgate fish porter for most of his adult life.

Jim was the son of James F. Flanagan and Alice G. Chapman, Micky's grandparents who died 6 and 7 years respectively after Micky was born. He was one of the children evacuated out of London during the Second World War to escape the bombing, a fact Micky later uses with fond recollection in his stand-up sketches and often refers to his dad finding it difficult to go for a few minutes in conversation without mentioning that he was an evacuee.

Jim was just nine years old at the time the Second World War started and on 1 September 1939, two days before the Declaration of War, the evacuations, in an operation named 'Operation Pied Piper', began. The British government decided to evacuate children from their homes in London, Coventry, Portsmouth, Birmingham and other vulnerable conurbations and he was one of the 800,000-plus kids who left their homes and families to avoid the air raids which were predicted for the big cities.

Once the war was over, Jim returned to his home in Bethnal Green and a few years later, a young lady called Sylvie Smith caught his eye. While Jim had been her first serious boyfriend, Sylvie, like most young women at the

time, enjoyed social evenings at the local dance halls and she would often spend a night there with her near-neighbours, the notorious Kray Twins. In fact, Micky later used these encounters between his mum and the infamous London gangsters as part of his stand-up material for his Out Out tour, years later, and in an interview he gave to the *Independent* in 2011, he revealed: 'I don't do dewy-eyed nostalgia, I really guard against doing a version of the Good Old Days when you could leave the front door open and Ronnie and Reggie would come in and torture you. My mum danced with them, the Krays, she did. Everyone says it but my mum really did. But she was also savvy enough to know; have a dance but don't walk home with them.'

Ronald 'Ronnie' Kray and Reginald 'Reggie' Kray were the biggest perpetrators of organised crime in the East End of London in the fifties and sixties and with their gang, 'the Firm', they were involved in armed robberies, arson, bribery and two murders. The twins were equally feared and respected in the East End district and as nightclub owners, mixed with celebrities like Frank Sinatra, Diana Dors and Judy Garland. They were arrested on 9 May 1968, 6 years after Micky was born, and sentenced to life imprisonment. But growing up in London in the years when the Krays were most celebrated meant that crime and law breaking filtered quite easily into the lives of the working-class men and women in the East End.

Micky's dad was not immune to the pull of making a

quick bob or two for his growing family and as Micky later recalled in an interview with the *Telegraph*, the boundaries between being a criminal and an ordinary working-class man dipping into the odd dodgy activity were less defined.

'I think, like a lot of men at the time who come from an east London background, Bermondsey background, it was easy to get sucked into low-level crime. He took chances, was unfortunate to get caught and ended up in prison. But he wasn't a "criminal". When you've got four kids and someone offers up the opportunity to get an easy buck you might just take it. The last time they locked him up he shaped up after. I think [prison] worked. He preferred beer, betting and sex to the slight riches the odd caper might bring.'

Growing up with his family on a council estate in Bethnal Green, Micky lived at number 48 Tomlinson Close, a small street off Brick Lane, with his three siblings: Patricia, the eldest, who was six years old when he was born; Terence, his older brother, who was three years older; and Lisa, who was just a year old when Micky came along. Sylvie had her children young and very close together, as was the norm in those days. She was twenty-two years old when she had Patricia, twenty-five when she had Terry, twenty-seven when she gave birth to Lisa, and twenty-eight when Micky completed the family. All the children were born in Whitechapel and all were very close, growing up in their cosy, inner-city home – Micky would share a box room

with his elder brother while his two sisters shared another room. The *Oxford Dictionary* definition of Cockney is 'a native of East London, traditionally one born within hearing of Bow Bells,' so the family can truly count themselves as bona fide Cockneys.

When, years later on one of his stand-up tours, Micky was asked about his 'Cockney authenticity' he responded with a reference to being born to the sound of the Bow Bells of the church, St Mary-le-Bow. In fact, in true cheeky Micky style he has been known to tell people that his mum was up and swinging on the bell of the church while she was in labour with him!

As a baby, his mum Sylvie thought he was quite 'plain' looking, not that she was worried. 'Plain or ugly in the cradle, good-looking at the table,' was one of her favourite sayings for her youngest boy. 'I wanted to give him back,' admitted his dad.

When he was a little older, Jim bought him his first bike. He was very pleased with the brand-new set of wheels for his youngest child and described it as 'a cracking bike'. But Micky only rode it once before coming off and landing on his face. He didn't ever want to get back on that bike, which made his dad cross. At the pub he would complain about his 'strange child' to his mates. 'Everyone falls off bikes and gets back on 'em. He was strange. And sullen.'

Growing up with three older siblings meant that Micky wasn't ever short of playmates to entertain him but he was a social, able little boy anyway and surrounded by

his neighbours' children on the council estate, there were lots of other kids to get up to mischief with, or kick a ball about. Footie became a game that was very much part of council estate identity and Micky and his Tomlinson Close team often took on their 'rivals' – the kids from Kirton Gardens. The Kirton Gardens boys didn't have a good enough 'pitch' to play on so would often come along to Tomlinson Close and play on theirs. Micky remembers that his team would frequently win and that he was often quite talented, with a long throw and the odd header.

The estate was the children's playground – there were no big designated play areas as such, back then – and the boys used to enjoy balancing on the wooden beams that would run along the side of the pavement. Micky was like any normal kid and enjoyed the challenges that his environment had to offer – walking along the wooden beam till there was a gap and then jumping to the next beam across the gap was always a challenge and one rarely completed by him and his pals. In fact, when he was about eight or nine years old, he tried to make the jump between the beams and ended up scraping the skin off his shin when he misjudged the distance and caught his leg on the next beam. Boys will be boys!

Micky went to school at the Columbia Primary School in Columbia Road and although a bright child, he wasn't always fully focused on school work and would find himself daydreaming most of his school days away. Also, he wasn't an overly 'happy' boy and the teachers often

reported back to the head teacher about him being a particularly 'miserable' child.

'You were the most miserable sod ever when you were younger,' his mum scolded Micky years later. 'When you went to primary school you were so miserable, the head teacher called me to the school and said, "Is everything alright at home, Mrs Flanagan? What's wrong with Mick?"'

While there wasn't anything wrong with Micky, he did come across as a very serious youngster and would rarely smile – certainly never in photos, Sylvie once revealed. He was also a bit of a daydreamer and had the ability to switch himself off from the hustle and bustle of a busy household and daydream the hours away. It was a personality trait that both his parents remember and his dad wasn't that impressed by his so-called 'idleness'.

Years later Micky recalled in a typical stand-up skit that their family set-up was fairly standard for the decade: men worked in physical jobs and went to the pub while the women stayed at home and raised the family.

'He was a good bloke, me dad,' recalls Micky in his *What Chance Change?* radio show on BBC4 Extra. 'Men in those days didn't do much round the house, though, did they? Back then, if he shut the cupboard door he thought he was helping out.'

As the youngest of the family, quite often Micky would be the one who went shopping with his mum and helped her out while his older siblings amused themselves or

went to school. There was one memorable trip to the supermarket with Sylvie he told listeners to his radio show, *What Chance Change?*, when his parents broke the law – or more specifically, his mum would half inch (Cockney slang for 'pinch' or 'steal') when they went shopping.

'I remember going to the supermarket with my mum and her telling me, "No, you can't have Alphabetti Spaghetti, it's too dear! You can't even spell it, you thick git!" And then, to add insult to injury, I realise she's put a stolen chicken in my sports bag and there's me trying to tell her that, "I don't wanna nick the chicken, Mum!"'

It was also a time when his dad was doing some dodgy dealings and storing questionable merchandise in the house. This was a prominent memory for Micky and he later recalled in a magazine interview (*Time Out*, 2006) how he found it odd that some of the products he was watching on TV, on a show called *Police Five*, (an early version of *Crimewatch*) were stuff he had seen piled up upstairs by his dad. Not only that, but as they were living in a fairly small council house, there wasn't much extra storage room so most of the illegal gear that was being 'looked after' by his dad was, in fact, being stored in Micky's bedroom.

'I appear to have spent most of my early years staring out of a window or lying on the grass, looking up at the sky. My mum reckons I was a thoughtful and sensitive boy. My dad said I was a miserable little bastard,' Micky revealed. 'I remember watching *Police Five* and Shaw

Taylor, the presenter, would show some recently stolen goods and he'd ask people to inform the police if they'd seen them. I was a confused eight-year-old. The stuff was up in my bedroom. My dad was looking after them for a friend. The house was always like that, like an episode of *Only Fools and Horses*. It seems he always hoped I'd be as easy with criminal activity as he was, but the thought never occurred to me. Sorry, Dad!'

Saying sorry to his dad about not following him into a life of crime and the obvious absurdity of his father wanting him to be a full-time criminal is an interesting paradox. On the one hand, a lot of boys growing up in the sixties idolised their fathers to such an extent they would do anything to please them – going into the family business, for example, or becoming a con 'like Dad' because there was no greater hero than a father: The man of the house provided for the family and so what if that meant things were a little shifty or from hooky street? 'Hooky' is a term used to describe stolen or otherwise dubiously sourced items; Hooky Street being where you can buy 'hooky goods'.

In an interview about his father years later, Micky apologised again for not following him into a life of (petty) crime and why, even though he was regarded as a disappointment at the time, he just didn't want to get caught up with anything illegal.

'A lot of the people I grew up with ended up as druggies or in jail and I learned from visiting my dad in prison that

you achieve nothing from crime so I walked away,' Micky revealed to the *Surrey Comet* in 2007.

When he interviewed his mum and dad about not being more of a thief when he was younger, both parents found it funny that their son didn't take to stealing – even when given such perfect opportunities to pilfer while working at a fish market – a job he took on after leaving school.

'Micky, you were so honest, you really disappointed us – you didn't even steal a winkle!' his mum told him in his BBC 4 Extra radio show. 'You did disappoint your dad by not being a thief. I had to rely on Terry and your dad to steal me some fish.'

His dad, who at the time of writing is eighty-four years old, also humorously pointed out the error of his son's ways to him when he participated in the same radio show. 'You were never a thief. There was so much skulduggery going on down there you could have earned a lot of money… Where you got that honest gene, I don't know.'

While a life of crime wasn't something to be condoned, Micky accepts that his dad was simply trying to do his best for the family and in his Back in the Game tour, he describes his childhood as not just being poor, but 'Africa poor' as an explanation for his father's less than 'strait-laced' approach to earning a living.

'By the time my dad was 26, he had kids, a council flat and a job on the docks,' he told the *Portsmouth News* in 2013. 'His life was more or less done.'

That wasn't to say that a young Micky didn't get up to the odd bit of mischief, however. Even though he might not have broken the law, both he and his mates still enjoyed getting into the odd spot of bother! One of the most memorable times was when he and a friend got their first glimpse of female flesh when they tried to spy through the curtains of their local pub. The Well & Bucket was on Bethnal Green high street and one evening, Micky and a mate followed his dad there. It was a night when there were strippers performing as the entertainment and the curtains were closed so only the punters inside could enjoy the sights. But a cheeky Micky saw an opportunity to spy through a gap in the curtains and with his mate's help in the shape of a leg-up, he was able to see the stripper through the gap at the top of the window. It was an experience he would never forget and a memory he shared with fans on his Back in the Game tour.

'I saw the stripper through a chink in the curtains. I saw her vagina. I saw her pluck out a pubic hair and drop it in a man's pint. Quality!'

Even though he was the youngest of the family, Micky took on a role of being a protective brother to his sisters, and they shared a close bond. He told Alan Carr in an interview in 2013 that his sisters were 'his best friends,' and as a consequence of growing up with them, he had a lot of female friends when he was older as he could befriend them without any ulterior motive. He and his eldest sister Patricia reminisced about growing up in the East End with

a mixture of happy, yet unsettling memories of the gloom of the area when they discussed their childhood years later on his *What Chance Change?* Radio 4 show.

'Growing up in the East End I think we were essentially happy, weren't we, Mike?' recalled Patricia. 'It was a happy, carefree childhood. I do remember feeling sometimes that on a lovely sunny day the sunshine would be almost wasted on such an area. There must be another place where the sun would be better to spend its time,' she added.

Micky agreed. 'I remember going on school trips outside of London, thinking why do I feel so much freer out here, and then when you were on the coach coming back into London there was a sense of gloom – it sort of descended on you.'

He later reminisced about life in the East End in his Out Out tour, more poignantly how his life has changed from the days he spent in the working-class area of his youth to today, where the lines have been blurred between the classes. Micky once told the audience of his Out Out tour that he finds the idea of himself now living in a 'very nice house in a very nice street, in a very nice area of London' a bit uncomfortable as he knows that not that far away are kids who are going through the same issues he himself dealt with when growing up. 'I can see them thinking, "Why have these people got lovely great gardens and I've got a balcony?"'

Micky charts his childhood with the differences that he now finds in modern London. His younger years, as

he recalls, were different with regards to social media, fashion and, of course, making phone calls. As part of his Out Out tour, the comedian regaled his audience with memories of what it was like growing up in a household with just one telephone.

In some of his early gigs and routine stand-ups he would rely on the technological advances that have taken place over the years to prove how memorable it was growing up having only one phone in the house. He would have the audience in stitches when he would refer to his mother being livid when the phone would ring after 8pm. Especially if it interrupted her favourite TV show!

Micky's job after primary school was to go and collect the paper for his dad in the evening, which a man would be selling outside the pub each night. Whether he was merely being a cheeky youngster or was just discovering that he could be funny, he would go up to the vendor each night and every few weeks or so would ask him if he was the 'paper man' to which the man replied, 'Yes.' Micky would then say, with a cheeky smirk, 'Watch you don't blow away then!' and run off. It was a joke he repeated every few weeks or so and the man would fall for it every time.

Even though his recollections about his childhood are all humorous anecdotes that resonate from being a working-class Cockney or East End lad, he is ready to admit that the boundaries are less defined nowadays, such as in an interview with www.entertainment.ie, where he

recalled: 'The difference is so unclear now. You would have to go to a university to look up the definitive answer. Maybe a slight difference in values and culture. Class was a lot more defined when I was growing up in that sort of Marxist sense in that the only thing we had to sell was our labour – the hard definition of being working class. Having no possessions, no money, but you had your labour to sell. Now you meet someone who claims to be working class as they bought their house in 1979 but it's worth half a million pounds.'

When it was time to go to secondary school, Micky, like most boys his age, would find it more of a means to end, knowing the inevitable would happen and he'd end up leaving school early to make a living. At secondary school, Daneford Comprehensive School, which is now known as Bethnal Green Academy, he spent his days in a 'cocktail of truancy and detentions.' It wasn't that he was a particularly disruptive pupil at school, but for boys his age, education just wasn't top of the agenda. He admitted that from the age of fifteen onwards there was only one destination for him to head to, 'The Birdy!' The Birdcage Pub was situated on Columbia Road, so a stone's throw away from the primary school in one direction and a short walk from Daneford School on Gosset Street on the other. 'Everything was possible when you were in there – beer, women, everything!'

He lived just around the corner and from the age of fifteen, he would be coming in there over the next 30 years.

It wasn't a pub that was particularly known for trouble but had regulars who had either served time in prison or were about to go there. Micky remembers being in the pub with his dad one Sunday lunchtime and being introduced to a man called 'Red Face Tommy' who had just served 15 years in prison for 'going to work on the pavement.' It was an expression that Micky didn't understand but didn't dare admit to Red Face Tommy, so he just nodded his head. Only when he asked around a bit later did he discover that the phrase, 'going to work on the pavement', was a euphemism for being a bank robber.

It was in the classroom, messing around with his classmates, that a young Micky first got a taste for entertaining his friends through comedy, realising that making his mates laugh not only felt good but gave him a level of confidence too.

'My introduction to making people laugh was in school, whether it was messing about or just telling jokes. But being funny with friends and being funny on stage is slightly different,' he told *GQ Magazine* in 2013.

In one rather controversial skit on *Mock The Week* years later, Micky recalled an experience with a Nigerian-born teacher who would hit the boys with a ruler if they were being unruly. *Mock The Week*, a popular BBC panel show, invites six comedians each week to debate and discuss the stories that have been making the headlines that week, mostly political or sporting topics. Irish comedian Dara O Briain is the host and Micky has

appeared on the show, at the time of writing, eight times. (More on Micky's appearances on *MTW* later.) He caused controversy when he told the story of being punished at school by his Nigerian teacher, Mr Thompson. Micky put on an African accent to tell the tale, which aired in series 10, episode 4 of the show, and the audience reacted with a mixture of laughter and shock when he tried to mimic the African accent.

'The teacher would say, "'old out your fingerteeps," which we did, and then he would whack at 'em with a ruler.'

Speaking about the controversy later that year, Micky was keen to point out that he wasn't being racist or disrespectful and those that know him best are also quick to point out that he is anything but racist.

'I think there is just a knee-jerk reaction to any accent on TV because people straight away hear *Mind Your Language* or Benny Hill, or something and think we're going back to the 1970s,' he commented after the show in an interview with entertainment website Digital Spy. 'What I hope is that people are grown up enough now to know that my school teacher, Mr Thompson, was from Nigeria and that was his accent. I'm not being disrespectful or racist in repeating his accent, I'm just repeating his accent. Can we all be grown up enough now to say that's how he spoke? If all you're hearing is "He must be a racist because he spoke in a Nigerian accent", you're wrong. Let's have a grown-up approach. If I was to jump up and

down every time I heard a Cockney accent used to more or less imply that someone was thick and feckless, I could complain every single day of the week.'

While he openly admits that he wasn't exactly the best-behaved pupil at the school, he was a bright teenager with strong ideals and was strongly influenced by what was happening in the city around him. The seventies was a traumatic time for many Londoners, as changes in global trade disrupted a wide sector of the economy and Micky saw his dad lose his job as a docker when, during the decade, more than half of the inner-city docks closed down and their workforce fell to under 10,000, a third of what it had been 20 years earlier. Unemployment in London rose from 196,000 people (3.6 per cent of the workforce) in 1971 to nearly 400,000 (7.2 per cent of the workforce) in 1976. The economy had no more serious impact on Micky other than seeing his father go from a life as a docker to working at Billingsgate fishmarket but there was also a mood of unrest too. One social commentator pointed out that the mood within London was bleak during the seventies and many people felt the city's best days were behind it.

The website www.20thcenturylondon.org.uk reveals: 'As docks and factories closed, so inner city London developed a landscape of dereliction and decay. The population was shrinking and unemployment was rising. Some people predicted that London was dying.'

During his teenage years, Micky described himself

in an interview with the *Independent* newspaper as a former 'Marxist-Leninist', who as a fourteen-year-old had joined the Labour Party Young Socialists group, and as an angry youngster took part in the first Anti-Nazi League marches in the late seventies. Ironically, in the year Micky was born, former fascist leader Sir Oswald Mosley was attacked as he marched through the streets of the East End with members of his anti-semitic Blackshirt group. Mosley was known principally as the founder of the British Union of Fascists (BUF) and was a Member of Parliament from 1913–31.

The Labour Party Young Socialists was the name of the youth section of the British Labour Party from 1965 to 1993. The Marxist-Leninist political ideology combines the scientific socialist concepts theorised by Karl Marx and Friedrich Engels and the theoretical expansions developed by Vladimir Lenin. It is an expanded form of Marxism that emphasises Lenin's concept of imperialism as the final stages of capitalism and shifts the focus of struggle from developed to underdeveloped countries. It was a popular theory for young men and women who felt that the ideology could be used by working and oppressed people in their struggles for liberation and the building of a new world – a classless social system with one form of public ownership of the means of production and with full social equality of all members of society.

Taking part in the first Anti-Nazi League marches was one of the last things young Micky did before leaving

school. He was showing great passion about inequality and oppression and by joining the ANL march showed that he was conscious of the extreme right wing and keen to show his complete disdain for such ideology. According to socialist historian Dave Renton, the ANL was 'an orthodox united front' based on a 'strategy of working-class unity.' The organised marches and Rock Against Racism rallies in 1978 showed that there were many people in London who were prepared to make a stand against prejudice and racism and Micky was proud to be of that group, an indication that his gag about his Nigerian teacher wasn't the least bit racist: Micky was just being Micky and telling a story in his own comical way. There was no edge to his comments.

Being proud of his roots, he later described what life was like as a Cockney youngster – readily admitting this as he was a true Cockney who enjoyed a traditional East End childhood. In one of his sketches that he performed in his Out Out tour, he told the audience more about his days at school to paint a humorous picture of his education. A gag that never failed to get several laughs was his description of the two Design and Technology departments at school and what they taught the pupils to make each year: 'My school had two big departments, it had a woodwork department and a metalwork department. We made ashtrays in the second year, bottle openers in the third year and prams in the fourth year.'

Micky was a bright pupil who was by no means a low-

ability child but the conditions in those days for young boys to thrive and go on to further education weren't in place and as such, school was just treading water, a chance to while away the days, messing around with your mates until you were old enough to leave. While his cheeky behaviour and naughty streak didn't make him popular with the teachers, he was a popular boy with his peers, using his natural ability as a joke-teller to keep his friends entertained. Obviously being the class clown was fine if you just had to use your wit to get through each lesson but the teachers weren't so appreciative of his humour and the disruption he caused in class.

'We just tried to make each other laugh,' Micky recalled in an interview with his former classmates in 2010 as part of his Radio 4 series. 'The key each day was to get as many laughs as you could without getting too many detentions and into too much trouble. There was always a bit of satisfaction about upsetting as many teachers as you could, too. If you could get to a point when they would get into such a rage they would attack another kid, you'd pat yourself on the back.'

Comprehensive schools in the East End were trying to bring their establishments up to national scratch but the problem, even though some structures were in place to raise the standard of education in the inner-city comps, was that young boys of that decade saw their future dictated largely by the profession their father or other male family members were in. Traditionally, boys followed their dads

into the family business or into the same trade as their relatives, as young lads from the same family would all be expected to provide for that family.

But that wasn't to say there were no opportunities for some of the children at the school to think more openly about their futures – openly in the sense of ambition, the idea that education provided the opportunity of a 'career' rather than just 'work'.

In his Radio 4 *What Chance Change?* show and subsequently on numerous occasions during his early stand-up routines and Out Out tour, Micky told the audience about the day a careers advisor visited their school. While most of his classmates were happy 'staring out of the window and doing f**k all,' one pupil, Gary Hutton, told the careers advisor how his great ambition in life was to drive a van.

'The school sent a careers officer to us in the third year and asked us what we'd like to do with our lives. And it turned out the most ambitious kid in the class was Gary Hutton cos he wanted to drive a van. He stood up and said; "I'm goin' drive a van." Well, we [the class] erupted. We shouted, "You dreamer, Hutton! No kid from this school has ever gone on to drive a van!" We continued to taunt him; "C'mon, Hutton, this school is 'ere to produce the people that carry the stuff to the van."'

It's a humorous recollection and somewhat embellished for the purposes of a good comedy sketch but there was an underlying truth to it. There was no great ambition for

the students at school, who weren't there through choice or yearning for an education, merely going through the motions before they could blag about their age or be old enough to work, out in the real world. And in Micky's class there really was a boy called Gary Hutton, who really did respond to the careers advisor with the now infamous words: 'When I'm older I want to drive a van.' Years later, Micky was interviewed about his old mate Gary and asked whether he knew what had happened to him. 'I dunno, I've heard tell he went on to do a number of different jobs but I don't know if any of them involved the giddy heights of driving a van,' he deadpanned.

School was deemed pointless by Micky and his pals and they couldn't see how certain lessons, especially science, could ever help them in life. It was a frustrating time for them and they felt there was little point in lessons like Chemistry, in particular. Why would a gang of boys like them need to learn anything about the periodic table, for example? It was a mystery to them at that age.

When asked what he wanted to be when he grew up, it surprised some of the teachers when Micky announced that he wanted to be a vet. But it was perhaps a more romantic view of the profession, rather than a legitimate desire to study and go to university that he found appealing after finding out the qualifications needed.

'I remember sitting there and saying to one of the teachers that I wanted to be a vet... then when he got back off the floor from laughing and sat back in his chair, I

remember him telling me all the qualifications I'd require, listing all the things I'd need to be a vet and I was thinking, "This ain't gonna happen, is it?" I just thought I'd need to know the difference between the right end of a cat and a dog,' Micky revealed as part of his 1980s segment on his Radio 4 show in 2010.

Nevertheless, there were lessons that a young Micky did enjoy. He liked sports and would excel at swimming, achieving a bronze swimming medal in a competition. He had been swimming at the local swimming baths since he was seven years old and during his Back in the Game tour, he revisited the swimming pool he used to frequent as a child, the York Hall Leisure Centre Swimming Pools. In addition to swimming, boxing was a hobby that he enjoyed, although he didn't take either sport to a competitive level. Coincidentally, York Hall was famous for its high-profile boxing matches and while Micky never boxed at the venue, he did have several bouts at Repton Boxing Club in Bethnal Green, one of the oldest established boxing gyms in the country, known for its motto, *Non viscera no gloria* – no guts, no glory.

'My mum didn't think I was completely committed to the sport, as rather than get me the whole kit, she just sewed a couple of red satin stripes down the side of my football shorts,' Micky revealed years later to viewers of his Out Out DVD.

Back to school and Micky wasn't ashamed to admit he left at fifteen with just 'a bronze swimming medal and an

ashtray.' At that stage, rather than be upset that he hadn't carried on with his education, he was ready to leave his school days behind him and embrace the working man's world. Others weren't quite so blasé about a young man giving up his education, though, and he found that a lot of people struggled to understand why he had decided to leave school with no qualifications when the subject came up in conversation. At the time he believed that his way forward in life was through work, and more specifically, work with his dad at the fish market, which would give him a good wage for a teenager. His perception of what was a good idea at the time was justified, but after years of hindsight he since realised that such a decision took him on a path that would close off many opportunities that having a solid education could bring. In his Radio 4 show he admitted to listeners that his decision to leave school at the time was, he thought, the best option for him. 'I thought I was making life very easy for myself. I didn't have the vision to think, "I am now sealing off a huge range of opportunities to go see the world," for example. I just thought, "Leave school, get a job down the fish market, meet a girl down the local pub, probably get her pregnant, go to the council and get a council flat, you're done." You could be twenty-one years of age and it's all over.'

This was what happened to his parents' generation and it was about to happen to Micky, leaving education as soon as you could to start earning a living and have a family of your own.

Years later, he interviewed author Paul Willis, who wrote a book in the seventies about how working-class kids got working-class jobs called *Learning to Labor*. Paul explained that in that era, boys of a certain age demonstrated a negative attitude towards academic work and tried to become part of a more adult world and thought that manual work was their lot in life. Though they may not have continued formal education beyond the minimal legal requirement, the lads recognized that as society was run by capitalism, there was no such thing as equality of opportinuty for them, and that no matter how hard they tried, success was largely reserved for middle-class students. Paul identified numerous similarities between the attitudes and behaviour developed by the lads in school and those on a shop floor at work, where having a laugh was a vital tool to deal with boredom, authority and repetitiveness.

The book was an important study on the seventies working-class classroom and had great relevance to Micky's life at the time as a young working-class schoolboy. He was oblivious to its conclusions, yet years later it would prove to have a pivotal effect on his life and his comedy. Class is a topic that Micky uses in his stand-up shows, certainly in the Out Out tour, as a way of defining his background and gives a sense of his life when society put a lot more of an emphasis on it. In one of his sketches in the *What Chance Change?* show he interacts with the audience and asks them to define what sort of class they think they

belong to. When he asks one lad, a guy called Will, why he believes himself to be working class, Will simply answers, 'Because I work.' It was a simple definition, and one that Micky then took up: 'People have been discussing this for hundreds of years and you've just summed up what it is to be working class, cos you work!' This whole topic of class was a subject he studied in depth when, before becoming a professional comedian, he returned to education and used Paul's book and the theories he discussed in a essay he did at the Open University about how he 'followed the pattern of his parents'. He also invited Paul onto his BBC Radio 4 show to discuss the theory, 'why working class children get working class jobs'. Paul made some interesting observations about Micky's education and the success he had become.

'Can education lift all kids like you, Micky?' he asked the comic. 'Your saving grace is your humour, time and time again. Would you have done better if you had worked hard, got your GCSE and gone on to higher education at sixteen? No, you've got that informal culture. That's what made you.'

'I made the mistake of following my family of no qualifications so I can identify with the book,' confirmed Micky in response to the question. He continued to share his decision-making process with Paul and the listeners of his Radio 4 *What Chance Change?* show. 'When we all left school we all went fairly quickly with no qualifications into work. We lied about our ages, to get down the market

and start working.' He told the story of the time that someone from the school board came round to his home and annoyed his mother by knocking too loudly on the door. She then told the school board officer that as Micky now had a job, he should be left alone. Mrs Flanagan certainly wasn't afraid to stick up for her son!

Micky and his school mates, among them Huey Benjamin, Colin Woolfe and Tony Rosen, were all the same age and all left school early with no qualifications. The friendships they made in school were solid and years later they reminisced about how funny it was to be at school, and how 'pointless' going to school was.

'There was no driving force in school,' chuckled Tony Rosen to Micky. 'I remember sitting next to Gary when he said he wanted to drive a van. That was it, we all just wanted to get out and get working. I wanted to wear an overall and come home covered in crap to show that I'd been working, that's all I wanted.'

The group of lads was close and Micky would find himself socialising with his mates after leaving school, often in the local boozer even though they were underage. 'We went out drinking quickly after leaving school. We were down the pub on a regular basis by the time we were fifteen or sixteen, down the Halfway House.'

The Halfway House on Hackney Road was another typical East End pub – rough round the edges and comprised mainly of locals seeking solace in a pint after a long day's graft. When Micky appeared on *The Jonathan*

Ross Show years later, he admitted to the host that he and his mates actually started drinking at fourteen years of age and having lock-ins in local pubs was a regular occurrence.

'It was a given! I remember I was with me mates down there one Wednesday night. We all ended up drinking there till about 1am and then the police turned up and they kicked the door in, put us all against the wall. They wanted names and our ages and you're a bit drunk and say, er, Billy Bunter, 7/10/68... That made me ten years old. But actually they done us all a favour as we all had school in the morning.'

But on leaving school they were now working men and deserved a working man's drink in the evening. For Mick, it was an exciting new chapter in his life, one of work, booze and girls.

'That was the beginning of the end,' he recalled in a 2006 interview with *Time Out*. 'Booze and sex. A girl hinted that she'd wank me if I bought her a Wimpy and chips. It was deemed good to have a girlfriend on your arm, especially if she was tidy. Saturday night was the girls' night, Friday night was the lads' night.'

But while ogling other girls was all part and parcel of being a lad in those days, Micky was very protective of his elder sister, Patricia, when she started coming to the pub, too. He wasn't happy if the blokes he was with started to wolf whistle at her and made sure everyone knew he was his sister and off limits!

Patricia recalls: 'I remember walking into the pub and your face was like thunder and you said to me, "Do you realise every bloke in the pub is looking at you?" You weren't happy, Mick!'

'I do remember, if I was ever in the company of men who didn't know who you were, I would always say very quickly, "It's me sister, it's me sister," I had to get that bit in before they could say, "Cor, look at that! I'll have some of that!" I didn't want them to say the sort of things men say to me sister!'

Patricia appreciated that her youngest brother was just taking on the role of a protective big brother but that didn't stop her making fun of him when the friends she was with asked if she knew the bloke with black curly hair.

'It's funny, though, Mick, cos I spent most of the time in the pub saying to my friends, who asked me if I was your sister, I was like, "No, oh my God, no, I don't even know him!"'

It's obvious to see that being cheeky and funny ran in the family and there were fun times ahead for Micky and his mates. Entering the world of work meant they were deemed adults in other respects, such as being able to often attract girls who were impressed with their working men credentials. But his first job, at the fish market in Billingsgate, was no easy ride…

Chapter 2

SCHOOL STORIES AND
FISH TALES

'Up at 'alf five? You're 'avin' a giraffe, Dad!'
Cockney definition: 'giraffe' (noun) laugh

The alarm went off at 4.30am and Micky groaned. Working life for him began at that time of the morning and it was tough for a teenager. The white overalls went on and then it was time to get to the market for the 5.30am start, a time when most other teenagers were still dreaming away their adolescence, tucked up in bed.

Micky recalled some amusing anecodotes from his time at the fish market and shared them with his listeners on the *What Chance Change?* radio show. It gave the audience a peek at what working life was like for the fifteen-year-old. It was a tough job but one that Micky did without complaint, even though he really didn't like getting up so early.

'I miss the times and the banter,' he revealed on his radio show, 'but I don't miss getting up at half past four. Not that I did get up that quickly. Me dad used to come in, turn the light on and I'd just get up and turn it off. Then he'd come back in and keep turning it on and off!'

Working at Billingsgate was in those days a very promising job for a youngster like Micky but he was only able to get such an opportunity because his dad already worked there – bringing your son into your place of work so he could begin his career as a grafter was the norm back then, and Jim was even able to help a couple of Micky's mates start work there as he could 'vouch' for them.

'When I left school I came to work with you down the market, then I went on to get the fish porter's licence when I was seventeen, didn't I, Dad?' Micky recalled in the on-air interview with his father in 2010.

Jim replied: 'Yes, it was considered a very good job. You only got it cos I was working there and that's how you got into it. No one else got in – OK, some of your mates did, but it was only sons of the workers who got in.'

'It was very much a father-and-son thing,' Flanagan junior recalled. 'To get in the fish market you had to have a brother, an uncle or a father working there. It was quite funny, walking behind him, my feet dragging along Liverpool Street for the 5.30am start. That was tough when you're a teenager.'

Originally a general market for corn, coal, iron, wine, salt, pottery and fish, in 1699 an Act of Parliament was

passed, making it 'a free and open market for all sorts of fish whatsoever'. Until the mid-nineteenth century, fish and seafood were sold from stalls and sheds around the 'hythe' or dock at Billingsgate. As the amount of fish traded increased, a purpose-built market became essential and in 1850, the first Billingsgate Market building was built in Lower Thames Street but it was demolished in 1873 to make way for a bigger, better building, which still stands in Lower Thames Street today. (It relocated to the Docklands in 1982.) This was where Micky began his working life, making his way to the market every morning, and he enjoyed his early years, working hard. The market was beginning to shrink by the end of the seventies owing to supermarkets beginning to dominate the supply chain but the atmosphere among the workers always created a buzz – it was constantly cheery, loud, full of banter and camaraderie, and Micky loved working in such an environment.

'I certainly remember being surrounded by a lot of funny people growing up, by people who were odd, hilarious, quirky and genuinely funny men. I was surrounded by all these types of men at the market – they would be good at banter, they were very, very funny men,' Micky explained in a 2013 interview with entertainment.ie.

Micky did so well at the market, as a fish porter and as a stand boy, which saw him 'boiling and measuring various shellfish' that in 1981 he gained his Fish Porter's Licence, something that meant he began to earn a terrific wage

for a young teenager. Having a licence was a prestigious accolade and given to porters by their superintendents if they showed 'good character and fitness'.

'In 1981 I had reached the dizzy heights of being a Billingsgate fish porter,' recalled Micky to *Time Out*. 'They didn't let just anyone do this, you had to have a licence.'

'I was Billingsgate fish porter 279, Licence to carry cod,' confirmed Micky in his Out Out tour. 'I was earning £250 a week in 1981. That was a footballer's wage! At the age of seventeen, I had peaked in terms of my career.'

But rather than be content with his promotion and exceptional wage, Micky was beginning to feel despondent about life and the daily slog at the market, longing for a new direction to head in. It wasn't an easy thing to admit as he knew that if he left his job he'd be hard pushed to find something else that would earn him the same pay, but he was becoming fed up with the daily grind.

'I got the licence but this is where it all starts... this is where it all starts to unfold cos I'm not happy. I want more. It was all a bit bleak,' he told an interviewer for *Time Out* magazine. 'Getting up at 4.30am in the morning, pulling fish up a hill in the pouring rain. Going home and watching that film, *Saturday Night and Sunday Morning*. I had that working-class anger in me; I wanted more from my life.'

Discussing his decision with his family meant that he had to bear the brunt of his parents' disappointment but

he was adamant that life wasn't going to be all about fish. Both Sylvie and Jim were surprised at the decision and his mum especially thought he was being 'over dramatic'.

'I was surprised. I was disappointed, I thought you had a job for life there and you left. You turned in your badge,' his dad told him, years later, when they discussed the decision Micky made in the early eighties. 'Apart from being a good job wage wise, you had got the chance to go and get another job too, cos the hours were so good. You could have been a taxi driver or anything. Was it something we said that made you leave?'

His mum was equally unimpressed by her son's decision to leave the job and made sure he knew how she felt – this was a woman whom Micky has said would regularly threaten him with a knife if he was naughty, so he knew he'd be in trouble.

'It was disappointing, not that you nicked any of the fish, anyway,' Sylvie revealed in a conversation with Micky and Jim, broadcast on Radio 4 in 2010. 'Your dad didn't know what to tell people in the changing rooms when they asked him why you weren't nicking the fish. That was another thing he was disappointed in!'

But Micky reckoned he had a good defence for not pilfering the fish while working at the market as he regularly gave his employers a bit of lip if they weren't polite to him. By stealing from them, he reckoned he wouldn't be able to be as cheeky as he was.

'If I nicked the fish, I didn't think I'd be able to talk

to the governors the way I did. They would boss me about and say, "Go and get those boxes over there," and I would say, "Don't you say please and thank you?" And they would be, "Oh, here we go."'

But it seems that excuse didn't hold much weight with his mum, who told him: 'They wouldn't have worried about you nicking the fish anyway, everyone was doing it, including them!'

But Micky had made up his mind and, fed up with the doom and gloom of London life, he decided he needed a brand new start – and he wouldn't be making it in this country, either. He wanted to head to America.

'It felt bleak to me – the East End, beyond all the "Knees Up Mother Brown" stuff, all people did was work their nuts off, live in the worst housing and be sent to the worst schools. I wanted more from my life,' he told listeners to his 2010 Radio 4 programme.

One freezing January morning he decided enough was enough and started planning a new life in New York. The idea had come from a fellow fish porter who knew how disgruntled Micky had become and suggested he went away to New York for a year. He gave him the name of a guy who ran a restaurant and bar on Fire Island, a seaside resort close to Long Island, and told him to try his luck.

'I was seventeen and I was pulling fish up a hill, thinking, is this it? All my friends were bedding down but I wanted more from my life so I ran off to New York,' he told a *Time Out* interviewer in 2007. 'When I

got to New York, it turned out the guy I was meeting had arrived there 20 years earlier from Bethnal Green on the run from the police.'

The decision to head to the Big Apple was one that changed his life, but his parents, even to this day, were still perplexed as to why their second son had to make such a drastic decision.

'In my mind it was either to get away from a bird or the law. And you would never level with me,' his mum scolded years later when they discussed his move abroad on *What Chance Change?* 'It does sound terribly dramatic doesn't it, though. You know what they say about women being drama queens? You're a drama king, Mike! You were a very dramatic seventeen-year-old.'

But Micky was adamant about going, and no-one could change his mind. He had grown to loathe the place he lived and was feeling trapped by the montonous routine of work and going to the same pubs with the same people. Still young, he yearned for a bit of adventure, which was a very brutal but honest admission.

'These feelings, I couldn't help how I felt and I knew the one thing I could do was to run away. I had seen *Saturday Night Fever*. I was completely empathising with Tony Manero, and in 1981 I bought a one-way ticket to New York City,' Radio 4 listeners were surprised to learn.

Having earned a good wage at the market, Micky funded his own plane ticket and at seventeen, 'ran off to New York' in search of a new start.

New York was a buzzing place to be for a young Englishman in the eighties. On the outside, the city wasn't too different from London – the streets were filled with people with big dreams and hopes, the subway trains decorated top-to-bottom in graffiti and the Mayor of New York, Edward I. Koch, was trying to get the crime rate down as the crack epidemic threatened to spiral out of control. But while there were not big contrasts to be made on the outside, Micky found the people to be completely different to the working-class men and women he was used to being surrounded by. While New Yorkers are known for being the most friendly of folk, it was their collective level of OTT politeness and optimism that Micky found surprising and while he found it endearing at first, it soon began to grate. Speaking about his experience across the pond, the comic has fond memories, which he was happy to share in a broadcast with his Radio 4 listeners.

'It was quite a big thing to do in the eighties, we didn't travel very far in the sixties and seventies, I was a naïve seventeen-year-old. But the place was buzzing. People would talk about their futures whereas England was a horrendous, bleak place to live in the early eighties. There was a lovely dose of positivity and naivety and craziness and excess. I have a love/hate relationship with New York, it's a very challenging place because they are very competitive, the Americans.'

One of his strongest memories of being in the States is being on his own in his hotel room and watching one of

the strangest things he'd even seen on TV – The National Standing Championships. Micky couldn't believe that a country could run such a bizarre competition but he was transfixed. He made sure he kept watching until the end and discovered that the eventual winner had been standing for three days! It was pretty impressive, but he was quite sure that a good ol' British builder would take the crown if they kept the cups of tea coming!

Working in America was pretty much the same slog it had been in England. Washing plates for a living wasn't exactly what Micky had in mind, in terms of a career, but his year out in America did give him an important life-learning experience. And he knew that when he returned home he would need to make some changes.

Making a permanent move to America wasn't ever something that tempted the youngster, who admitted in an interview with the *Telegraph* in 2013, 'I love America because I don't have to live there. If you forced me to live there I'd go mental.'

More recently, he has said he can't imagine living anywhere but London now, possibly showing that his young adventures in another country helped him realise that the grass isn't always greener but it was an essential learning experience for him.

'Would I ever move out of London? I'm sorry, I don't understand the question – is there a life outside of London?' Micky asked when questioned by website www. entertainment.ie. 'I love London. I played with the idea

of it and I've come very close to it, but I end up looking in the mirror and saying, "You're a Londoner and this is your home." Sometimes, when the noise and grime gets too much, I do think about a little coastal village but I don't think I could do it. I need the sound of sirens before I sleep.'

The other big reason for him to return to England after spending the year working as a dishwasher and then 'prep chef' in the restaurant was that he was finding the American sense of humour lacking – specifically in areas of micky-taking that we do so well in Britain.

'We do a few things properly in the UK,' he explained on the *What Chance Change?* show. 'Taking the piss for one. It's frowned on a bit over there. Americans don't have the same sense of humour, do they? And it starts to get you down. Your micky-taking skills start to dwindle when you're out there and it rubs off on you. You weaken. Stuff goes by, you'd see something that you'd normally rip to shreds and you think, I'd normally have that, but you don't. And they don't drink as much as they should either, or skive.'

So in 1982, he packed up his things and caught a flight back to the UK, determined his life would now be different.

Margaret Thatcher, who became Prime Minister in 1979, had a lot to do with Micky's change in career: as soon as he returned home, he claims to have been influenced by the Thatcherite mood that was sweeping the country –

one of belief in the polices of monetarism, privatisation and self-help promoted by the Prime Minister herself.

The shift in working ideals, of making money for yourself, was something Micky decided to embrace and he started his own furniture business with a friend, telling Radio 4 listeners this wasn't such a good idea after all.

'So I came back from the US, it was the early eighties and I was caught up in that Thatcherite thing, when we all suddenly thought, "I'm going to be an entrepreneur." And a friend of mine and I, we opened up a furniture shop. We did very, very well for about four years and then very badly for the next four. We lost the business and I went back to live with my mum in the East End, which wasn't easy.'

Moving back in with his parents was, in the end, only a short-lived arrangement, mostly thanks to Micky's determination to make his own way in the world and so he bought himself a bedsit – and not a council bedsit, he is keen to point out. He charts the eighties as 'not one of the worst decades in the world', mostly because he became an 'international lover and player.'

He still enjoyed going out with his mates to the pub and was very close to the lads he went to school with, meeting up with them on a Saturday night as Friday night was the night you spent 'with your bird'. Two of his friends had married in their early twenties, mirroring their parents' pattern of getting a job, getting married and having kids and doing it while you were very young.

'I was twenty-one when I got married, and I married my first girlfriend,' Huey confirmed to Micky when they discussed meeting girls on the radio show. Tony agreed. 'You were twenty-one or twenty-two and you got a girlfriend, then a car, then kids. Our parents all got married very young; my mum was married with four kids at twenty-five. It wasn't like they were saying, what are you doing, why are you getting married so young? It was the norm.'

But Micky, who had escaped the 'traditional' route of marrying young after going to America for a year, was now enjoying life, as he put it, as an 'international playboy'. The flat he owned was basic, but for a twenty-two-year-old single man it was a dream come true. He had a stereo hi-fi unit that he kept on the floor of the living room, a small kitchen and a futon that doubled up as his bed. He wasn't awkward with the ladies and quite often brought them back to his bedsit after a date on the Saturday night. In his Out Out tour, he recalls one such evening and the number of things he did to impress a woman. The whole situation of taking a woman out on a date formed a big part of his act and Micky knew how to tell the story well. It was a simple, laddish tale about how he thought at the time he was an 'international player', a man who had a way with women and knew how to treat them well. When performing this part of his act on stage, it wasn't just the men who would guffaw at the image of Micky only taking a woman out on a Saturday night ('all

men know that it's lads' night on a Friday, don't they?') and treating her to a steak dinner and a few cocktails. And if she was really lucky, she could have a prawn cocktail for a starter! The women in the audience would giggle as much as the men and it would help Micky set himself up as a man who had 'been there, done that' and was happy to relieve the memories.

'To sleep with a woman back then you couldn't just take her out for a few drinks, you had to wine and dine her. It was 1984 and if you wanted to impress a woman you'd present her with prawns on top of lettuce in a wine glass. I would take her back to my bedsit and I would go off and slip into the uniform of the international player, which is the silk black kimono. I've turned round to reveal the dragon, come back with a bottle of Blue Nun and nine times out of ten this was unsuccessful.'

Micky's 'uniform of an international player' was a long-running item in his later gigs and one that audience members who were the same age as the comic could identify with in the eighties. It had so much notoriety that years later, in an interview in 2013, a journalist from www.entertainment.ie asked if he still owned his now infamous dragon kimono. The reply was of course, yes!

'It's upstairs in the loft. You never know, if I end up single again, I may have to take it out of retirement. The dragon's got to come out.'

Micky describes himself as managing to 'pull birds' easily in the eighties but by the end of the decade he

had given his womanising ways a bit of a rest and had committed to living with one woman, a long-ish-term girlfriend, and he did everything in his power to impress her. But, as he admitted on his 2010 Radio 4 show, like most men, he found it a completely different experience – living on his own as a carefree bloke and living with a woman were two separate experiences altogether.

'I lived like a simpleton, really. I had a flat, I went and got a telly, a bed and a cooker for show; I kept my takeaway menus in it [the cooker]. Then, when you are living with someone, things become an issue. Making the bed can become an issue – the two pillows you bought are not enough, you have to have more and then all of a sudden, a cuddly toy appears on the bed. I like the light bulb myself but most women like the candles, they like living in a medieval monastery, don't they?'

It was a stand-up skit from his Out Out tour and one that held particular resonance with the men in the audience who could all relate to the experience of first living with a woman. But while his personal life might have been going well, Micky was suffering from a severe lack of confidence when it came to his career and was becoming increasingly frustrated at the jobs he was doing. It wasn't helped by the idea that being a working-class fella from the East End held a certain stigma. He was convinced that as soon as people knew he was a Cockney, future employment possibilities were shut to him and on his radio show in 2010 he cited that the Cockney darts player, Eric Bristow,

didn't help matters. Eric's professional darts name was 'The Crafty Cockney' and while that went down well for one of the best dart players of his time, Mick felt that his stage name wasn't giving those with a similar Cockney identity an easy ride.

'So here we have "The Crafty Cockney", perpetuated by Eric Bristow, the darts player. But honestly, how crafty can you be as a darts player? Will he try and get away with throwing four darts or something? 240! It did give us a bad name.'

By this time, towards the end of 1988, Micky was trying to pick up work wherever he could and got a job as a window cleaner. It wasn't a big career move, more a case of filling a gap while he decided what direction to take his life and it was a job that he loved. Why? The simple answer was that it allowed him to delve into other worlds and observe what was happening. It certainly appealed to his inquisitive nature, as he told the audience on his Out Out tour, years later. In some of his early stand-up performances, he would describe how he would love staring into the windows of people while they worked, office blocks in particular, and look in on them having meetings. He reasoned that his love of watching people at a meeting was that there weren't many business-meeting opportunities if you were working class so the whole process fascinated him – employees taking notes, trying to look interested, for example. It was a simple, everyday observation but the way he told it, it instantly became a

laugh-out-loud situation when he told it in his many early stand-up gigs:

'I used to have a sneaking suspicion that the excitement was all about the biscuits. When the biscuits come out there is a real buzz in the meeting room and all of a sudden the speaker wanted to get a shifty on as he wanted some of the custard creams and didn't want to be stuck with the garibaldis. Paradise used to be when I worked at the window cleaners. In the morning we'd get a break and have a lie down in the kitchen for a bit. I remember thinking, "It doesn't get much better than this."'

But while he used humour to lighten the situation, Micky felt the real reason he was struggling in his life was the fact that he had left education so early, without any qualifications. It wasn't a big worry for his peers, who were happily married or content with working at Billingsgate Market, but Micky had experienced a different world when he visited New York and he was now keen to try and make a better future for himself. It proved a turning point in his life and in 1989, 12 years after leaving the classroom it was time to head back to school.

Chapter 3

THE CORRIDORS
OF POWER

'I couldn't control the dustbin lids,
I was elephant's trunk every day.'
Cockney rhyming slang definition: dustbin lids (noun) kids;
elephant's trunk (adjective) drunk

After getting into terrible debt trying to make it as an entrepreneur with his furniture business, Micky's decision to go back to school would, he believed, offer him a chance to better his future and give his confidence a much-needed boost. While he might have come across to those who knew him as a cheerful, self-assured fella, the real Micky had long ago resigned himself to the idea that he didn't feel 'equal' to those who had an education. In fact he felt so inadequate, he didn't believe he had the intelligence even to converse with people who had finished school and received a full education. It was a big admission

on his part, especially when he opened up about it to listeners of his Radio 4 show, confessing that he would often feel 'insecure'.

'I would often feel insecure, before I even opened my mouth, that I would say something wrong or say it wrong,' he admitted. 'You get a little uncomfortable when you're amongst educated people; it's a feeling of being frustrated. It always bothered me that I didn't have an education, I think it affected my confidence and I decided this would be the time to do it.'

Micky visited his local Institution of Higher Education in Bethnal Green and enrolled to do a GCSE in English. It was a turning point in his life and rather than try and get his qualification as quickly as he could and get the hell out (as he did when he was at school), his passion for learning was ignited and he didn't want to stop.

'I decided to do GCSE English partly because it always bugged me that I left school with nothing. I blamed that on my background, growing up in the East End, where education isn't that important,' he recalled on his Radio 4 show. 'We did as little as possible in school. The minute I could, I walked out of the place. Us kids, we had a very anti-intellectual stance back then, you would quickly alienate yourself by answering a teacher's question.'

With a GCSE under his belt and a desire to learn more, he then saw the chance to enrol with the Open University when he spotted posters about a new initiative

that encouraged adults back into education. It was called Fresh Start and in 2010 he caught up with the teacher, Les Clency, whom he met in 1990 and who encouraged him to sign up. Les asked Micky what he'd been doing for 14 years after leaving school for there was never any doubt that he had the capability to stay in education, had he chosen to do so. But returning to school was an even braver move, argued Les, adding that he didn't let his frustrations get the better of him.

So in 1991 he was enrolled in the Open University and recalled how, in his Out Out tour, he enjoyed uni life: 'I decided to study with the Open University, which was fantastic as basically, you just had to get out of bed, put the telly on, make a cup of tea and watch the telly. I was doing that anyway, I might as well do it at an advanced level!'

He then went on to apply and be accepted on a Social Sciences and The Arts course at City University when he was twenty-nine years old. Even though times had moved on greatly since his days in the classroom as a disruptive teen, Micky still picked up on the sense of 'not belonging' when surrounded by his fellow students. Again, it was down to his belief that as a working-class East End boy, his fellow students and the lecturers would not take him seriously.

'It was still quite an unusual thing back then for working-class kids to go to university. The accent would cause a few problems. I would speak out in the lecture

and everyone would think, "Blimey, the window cleaner's keen, isn't he?"'

The audience would laugh at Micky's recollections of such a tale when told on his Out Out tour, but with every gag, there was a palpable sense of achievement, too. Here was a Cockney charmer returning to mainstream school and shrugging off any so-called snobbery with a joke

But whatever his fellow students thought of him, he was successful in university life and was awarded a BA. He marks the occasion in usual Micky fashion when recalling his new qualification. For him, getting this degree meant he had taken a very real step out of the 'working class' world, into the realm of the 'middle classes'. And how did this imaginary step into middle-classdom present itself in a physical way? Well, it was all about the type of newspaper he then started to read. Before he returned to mainstream education he would pick up the red top tabloid, the *Daily Mirror*, and flick through it in under 15 minutes. Now, he would go for the more weighty paper, the 'multi-layered papers', as he told the audience of his Out Out tour.

'I was crossing over slightly into being in a middle-class world, an intellectual world. You can tell that by the newspaper I started to get. I used to get the *Daily Mirror* and be done in 15 minutes but in the middle-class world, where if you've got a degree, you've got to be one of life's thinkers; therefore you need to get one of the big papers. The multi-layered papers.'

It is a light-hearted recollection of how he felt about his status at the time but life for Micky was changing and he was changing with it. It was perhaps no coincidence that he had developed a love of literature and his favourite book was *The Ragged Trousered Philanthropists* by Robert Tressell. The plot's biggest theme is about a class war – the politically powerless underclass of British society in Edwardian England being exploited by their corrupt employers. It tells the tale of a group of working men who are joined one day by a man called Owen, who has a just vision of society and launches several spirited attacks on the greed and dishonesty of the capitalist system. For Micky its themes hit home and the book had a profound effect on his thinking and reinforced a lot of his political views about how much the class system played a part in his own lack of education.

On discussing about his time at university with his mates, it was soon clear that they felt the same as him about leaving education early. One of them insisted that while his girlfriend wasn't as full of common sense as him, because she had a degree, she had the ability to earn double what he could ever earn. Perhaps this was one of the ideas Micky is so enthusiastic about – this idea of common sense being a useful life skill but one that doesn't come with a qualification.

'Imagine the people who, if they went to university, did a course on common sense? I'd be a winner. Some would come out and not be able to tie up their shoelace.

Common sense and enthusiasm gets you by in life,' he told his mates.

Fresh from uni, he still had bills to pay, however, and found himself back labouring on a building site with his school friend, Tony. He recalled on his Radio 4 show how much he had obviously changed during his university course without realising it. Suddenly, he wasn't the working-class lad looking out, he was the middle-class gent trying to get by in the working-class world. In an observation he made to listeners of his *What Chance Change?* radio show in 2010, he described how he was physically still very much part of his old working-class world but his brain was finding life fascinating and challenging, and he wanted to share his new world with his old mates.

'I went back to work on the building sites for a while and it was suggested that I didn't really fit in any more. I had started to read the big paper by now and my friend Tony pulled me to one side and said to me, "Look, you don't really fit in here any more, Mick. You know that discussion you tried to get started on globalisation, during the tea break. No-one is interested."'

It was time to find somewhere to channel his newfound love of learning and where better than back at school, as a teacher? It was an inspired decision for him: Micky hadn't had the best education but he was determined to make a difference in the lives of kids he could identify with and get them through the education system and give them a

future. So he embarked on a Postgraduate Certificate in Education (PGCE).

'I had seen the movies where a teacher comes in and changes the pupils' lives and they cheer you out of the classroom,' he said in an interview with the *Surrey Comet* in 2007. 'I thought I wanted to come out and help teenagers. So I signed up in the nineties for a PGCE. I thought I was going to help the kids so I went to the training institute in London and one of the bits they said to us that I remember clearly was be very serious in your first school placement, as the kids need to respect you. And as it's your first placement, don't smile before Easter. So when I got my first placement in an East London school I made sure I was very serious. You go in and you think, "Right, I am going to go in and help these kids, I'm going to change their lives."'

Micky recalled some of his experiences as a trainee teacher in gags that later formed part of his Out Out tour. In particular, he would like to tell the tale of trying to be a grown-up in a situation that a schoolboy Micky would find hilarious. For example, watching a child fall over in the corridor and finding it very difficult not to shout 'bundle!' at the top of his voice. Micky – or should that be Mr Flanagan in the classroom? – was trying to be an adult in a world still very much a childish place for him. He later admitted that he sought advice from the Institute of Higher Education, who provided him with a couple of action plans to help him cope with keeping control of

the children. In a hilarious sketch in his Out Out tour, he told the audience that he would employ several 'coping strategies' – namely, alcohol and drugs!

'I used to drink loads of vodka in the evening and in the morning I would take a Valium. By the time I used to get to the school I'm completely off my head. Controlling the kids was hard and the school they put me in had what they called an "inclusion policy" as well, which means you have a huge range of abilities in your classroom. You had the very bright students who I would give 10 hard questions to, and the not-so-bright, who I would let spin around on my chair.'

The audience roared with laughter as he told of his experience to a packed theatre in 2010 but the reality of the situation wasn't too different from the exaggerated picture he had just painted. He had gone into teaching believing that, after his own experiences in education, he would be in the perfect position to make a difference in the classroom but he was finding it far tougher than he ever imagined.

Micky was the first to admit that the idea of becoming a teacher was now not a realistic idea, especially as he was unable to keep control of the classroom without swearing at the students!

He described his teaching experience to entertainment website entertainment.ie in 2013 as 'the worst year of my life', explaining why, in the end, teaching wasn't for him: owing to a mixture of poor pay and hard work.

'It was too much work for what you got paid. Everything that was wrong about the school system when I was young was still the same. If you did a teaching training placement you would probably understand why thousands and thousands who do training to teach don't go on to do it. I think when I was doing it there was like a hundred thousand trained teachers who didn't teach. It's just too hard. The stress put on your average teacher is too high; the workload, the children, the school sizes, the class sizes.'

By now Micky was thirty-three years old and decided to put his teaching experience behind him by picking up work as a painter and decorator. Little did he know that it would be while working in this profession that his life in comedy would be about to start and very soon, his new role as a performer would overtake his job as a painter.

The break into comedy came when he noticed, a couple of years later, an advert on the TV (during a show that would be the equivalent of the daily topical programme, *The One Show*, these days) about a comedy course at Jackson Lane Community Centre in North London. It was a pretty random decision to make but Micky was always keen to expand his thinking and decided that as the course offered the chance to meet established stand-ups and hear about the circuit, it certainly would be worth a try.

'I remember thinking, "I would really like to do that,"' he confided in an interview with *GQ Magazine* in 2013, but it would be another year before he actually signed himself up for the course, putting it off because it 'seemed

like such a big jump'. And he has his girlfriend at the time to thank for persuading him to take the plunge as she 'badgered' him into doing it. A few years later he recalled in an interview with entertainment website, www.entertainment.ie, that he didn't think the lads he used to work with at Billingsgate would appreciate that he was going to learn how to make people laugh for a living, as they probably wouldn't remember him as a 'funny guy'.

'I wasn't the bloke down the pub getting everybody slapping their thighs so they will probably be a little surprised in that sense. It was when things got a bit more intimate and I got to know how to talk about things that people would find funny. The joker down the pub is often the last person you want to put on stage. It's the guy sitting in the corner, looking at the joke, thinking, "Why are these people laughing at this guy?"'

So Micky enrolled himself on the course – the nagging by his then girlfriend had paid off and by signing up for the weekly tutorials, the next biggest chapter in his life was about to begin...

Chapter 4

KNOCK, KNOCK.
WHO'S THERE? MICKY.
MICKY WHO?

'*Being funny with friends and being funny on stage is slightly different. What you're better off being is a really nice surprise, rather than a vague disappointment. So if you charm the club right, and you arrive there for your first unpaid gig and you do really well, the promoter will sit up and listen. And then you start getting booked.*'

GQ MAGAZINE

At thirty-four, Micky wasn't the youngest person to try his hand at comedy for a living, but what he lacked in youth, he made up for in enthusiasm and was keen to try a new direction in his life, believing it could be the start of bigger and better things. He wasn't a stranger to hard work either, and that's exactly what he did in the first few weeks of the course; he worked hard, he listened intently and he tried to soak up the information

and advice that was being given to him to allow him to take on board the skills needed to develop and try out material as a stand-up comic.

He recalled that one of the most important bits of advice that someone had given him on the course was that the art of writing stand-up material was just that, an art and a skill that didn't ever get easier over time.

'Someone told me very early on that the writing for new ideas never gets any easier and that's true. The other bits – the performance, the stage craft, the ability to deal with hecklers – that all gets easier and easier but coming up with new ideas, honing them and polishing them up stays the same as in the beginning,' he revealed in an interview with entertainment.ie in 2013.

But Micky was a quick learner and it wasn't long before he had gained enough confidence to impress the organisers of the course, and he was offered his first gig at the end of the placement by one of the women running the lessons.

It should have been a massive confidence boost – the course organiser who had probably seen hundreds of comic hopefuls in her time had chosen Micky for a gig. But while the organisers had no doubt about his ability to perform, he himself was fighting a lack of confidence and when the date came round for his first gig, he 'bottled it'.

'I couldn't do it,' he recalled. 'But she said, "You're never going to be ready, you know that, to do your first gig." So I booked in another one and then I went and did it.'

He then put his name forward for a few open-mic spots

in pubs and clubs and it gave him the confidence to think that, in 1996, when he performed his first gig, he could actually do stand-up. And do it well. But like any budding comic, the early years are filled with more bad gigs than successful ones, though they proved to be a learning experience all the same. Micky learnt quite quickly that a lot of the success, when you're just starting out as a comic, had to do with the venue you were performing at, as well as the material you had, and the audience you were performing for.

'If the environment's right, if it's a well-run night, the crowd are focused and they've paid a bit to come in, you find out quite quickly that you can do it. The difference is that you do so many disastrous pubs as well when you're in the early stages,' he disclosed when talking to *GQ* in 2013. 'You go in pubs where they are not listening, there's no investment and the sound's terrible. It's not your fault but that, combined with the fact that you're inexperienced, means that there's often a lot of terrible gigs early on.'

In one of Micky's early 'disastrous' gigs, the comedy had to be stopped due to a fire at the venue. In a room above a pub in Hanwell he had been struggling with a disgruntled crowd who were only half-heartedly listening so he was understandably over the moon when the fire brigade interrupted his set to evacuate the building. He told *GQ Magazine* in an interview in 2013 how he had hoped that the fire brigade would put a stop to the night

if the venue was still unsafe as he was struggling to get the laughs. Sadly for him, the fire crew allowed the punters back into the pub and he had to continue his set!

'The curtains caught fire at the back of the room, the fire brigade was called and they came and chucked us out. And I'm going round the car park, saying, "There's no way they'll let us back in," and I was quite relieved about that, to be honest. But then a fireman came out and said, "You can go back in," and my heart sank. I got a couple of laughs, which is what you hold onto in the early stages and that's when you think, "I want to get more." It was exciting, I remember that much.'

And Micky *did* want to get more. It was a buzz that was infectious and he needed to prove to himself that this new career was going to be the making of him. Inspired by some of the comics he grew up listening to – The Pythons, Peter Cook and Dudley Moore, plus some of the more modern stars at that time, like Eddie Murphy and Billy Connolly – he continued to work hard at writing and performing. Billy was a big influence on Micky's style. He had first seen him when he wasn't very old, in a pub in the seventies, long before Connolly became a mainstream comedian, a decade later, and from that point on, a national idol.

'I remember going to see him when I was very young,' he told the *Daily Record*, 'before the big comedy breakthrough of the 1980s. It was one of those "sit there beside him" gigs. I remember thinking it was such a skill. I

imagined being able to do that, keep people's attention for an hour and a half and make them laugh. I remember, even then, being more impressed by that than anything else – great sports people, actors, musicians and other people I was in awe of and from that day, it was my dream.'

Micky started honing his act and made sure he was getting gigs above pubs and in as many club spots as he could. He also decided to get as much experience in the comedy clubs as possible, not necessarily on stage himself but as an audience member, watching how other comedians performed. Harry Hill and Alexei Sayle were two of his favourites and he was inspired by how easy they made it look, and with this, coupled with the fact that more people were telling him how funny he was, he persevered.

In 1997, after just a few months on the circuit Micky decided to head to the Edinburgh Festival Fringe and take part in the '*So You Think You're Funny?*' competition, a chance for upcoming comics to showcase themselves in one of the biggest comedy festivals of the year. On reflection, it was a little premature for him to attempt such a prestigious show, but there was no doubting his enthusiasm for his newfound career and he was keen to experience as much as he could of the comedy circuit. Micky waited in the nearby Pizza Hut before he was due to go out and perform in the heats of the show, which was later won by Peter Kay. Although Micky didn't make it past the first stage, that did nothing to dampen his enthusiasm. And why should it? He was a new face and a

comic with fresh new ideas; he wasn't about to give up at the first hurdle.

The following year, in 1998, he took part in the *Hackney Empire New Act of the Year*, a long-running annual competition for comedy and variety acts that aimed to discover new stand-up and variety talent. It was a big opportunity for Micky to prove himself on the circuit. Chortle, one of the premier comedy websites in the UK, considered that the competition was 'a comedy institution' as 'past finalists have gone on to become household names. It presents the pick of the crop.'

Micky entered the competition having met the criteria that all entrants needed – he was 'seeking to become established on the live comedy circuit, was not yet a full-time paid professional act and had been performing for the obligatory one year'. He also brought with him the two recommendations from established promoters/agents/venues needed to take part in the competition.

Lee Mack, Ronni Ancona and Ardal O'Hanlon were all previous winners of the competition and Micky's nerves were stretched as he waited backstage to go and perform. His dad, Jim, was in the audience and willing his son to do well and as he sat through the seven acts of the evening, he had to admit that he found Micky quite impressive. There was another comic Jim liked that evening too, a tall, ginger-haired woman with a potty mouth called Catherine Tate, who had only just started, like Micky, on the comedy circuit in 1996.

Both Catherine and Micky found themselves losing out that evening – Hitchcock's Half Hour, a variety act comprised of Neil Cole and Tom Hillenbrand, took first place – but Micky's evening wasn't a total disaster. He came second!

His dad had some advice for him after the show and told him that his best bet to be successful was to put on a dress and do a drag act. Jim's uncle, also called Jimmy, was an entertainer and Jim told Micky that he was a famous drag act who used to entertain the troops. 'Put a frock on and you'll do better, Micky!' he recommended.

It wasn't a total disaster for Catherine Tate either of course, who later went on to become one of Britain's most successful female comedians and star in her own comedy series, *The Catherine Tate Show*, with her two most infamous creations, 'Nan' and 'Lauren'.

Buoyed by his runner-up position, Micky, who readily admitted he wasn't the most ambitious comic on the circuit, worked on his act, taking part in as many comedy nights as he could, trying to build up his experience in as many venues as possible. He was still working as a painter and decorator during the day but in the evenings, towards the end of the week, he would travel to open-mic nights and comedy gigs around the area.

'For about two years I'd be travelling to gigs with a bottle of white spirit in my bag so that I could clean the paint off my hands,' he explained in an interview with the *Portsmouth News* in 2013. 'But eventually I was doing

gigs every weekend and another comedian said to me, "If you don't quit your day job you won't enjoy either. Just take the rest of the week off, like the rest of us."'

It was advice that Micky was happy to listen to... giving up work during the day meant he could devote his time to honing his comedy act and making sure he had the best material to present to a crowd. And of course, it gave him a bit of spare time too.

'At first it felt like I had won the pools – getting up on a Monday and not having to work again until Thursday.' He was elated. But the work still had to be done, albeit in other forms, and with a fairly successful stint at the Hackney Empire New Act of the Year still fresh in his mind, he decided to accept a spot at The Comedy Store, just off Coventry Street in Soho, London. The only full-time comedy venue in the UK, The Comedy Store has played host to some of the biggest names on the circuit over the years, including Paul Merton, Robin Williams, Ruby Wax, Mike Myers, Julian Clary, Harry Enfield, Jack Dee, Eddie Izzard, Steve Coogan, Jo Brand, Lee Evans, Sean Hughes and Frank Skinner.

It was a Saturday night and Micky was due to take part in the Best in Stand Up slot, a regular show that happens every Thursday, Friday and Saturday. It is a 'classic' comedy show, in that a compere introduces four first-class comedians to the stage to do their thing while also having open spots in the act, a chance to see new talent on stage for the first time.

Micky was understandably nervous. He hadn't been gigging on the circuit for long and although he had been successful in performing for small crowds in pubs, this was a bit of a baptism of fire. Bob Hope once said that 'a laugh can transform almost unbearable tears into something bearable, even hopeful.' Sadly for Micky, he didn't get many laughs in his stand-up slot and marks his first ever gig at The Comedy Store as his 'worst death'.

'I think it really gave me a wake-up call that Saturday night,' he told *GQ Magazine* in 2013. 'I'd been offered a ten-minute spot too soon because I'd done so well in the Hackney Empire New Act of the Year. I went to The Comedy Store without the experience, the material and the tools to get through a tough comedy crowd. I went right down the pan. But apparently it's one of those things that almost everybody does. It's a really strange thing at the Store when the open spots come out because they're introduced as an act. There's none of that "Oh, give him a chance."'

The night was a disaster and Micky didn't return to The Comedy Store for another five years. Looking back, he reflected in an interview with the *Telegraph* in 2013 that the pressure on new comedians starting out seemed to be too high – and certainly too much exposure too soon wasn't a good thing.

'In a world that seemed to be speeding up in front of my eyes, there was a sense that if you had a little bit of ambition it had to be realised very quickly. What seemed

not to be in that equation was: what about the room to grow, to become as good as you can be before you're plonked in the spotlight? At the moment, someone with a little bit of talent is discovered, offered up, has their 15 minutes and then… "Next!" I didn't want that.'

It was 2000 and he was still relatively new to the circuit. Three years wasn't that long to get himself properly established and he readily admits that he didn't have the drive that some comedians did – those who were keen to promote themselves at every gig and try and get as much exposure as possible. Micky wasn't unprofessional when it came to turning up on time at gigs or cancelling last minute, he just wasn't pushing himself to do stand-up every minute of every day and openly confessed to not being the most driven newbie on the circuit. But then something changed. Keen to perfect his act, he had a steady stream of successful, small open-mic spots and had his confidence boosted on a number of occasions; but it was about performing for the bigger crowds that was to be the making of Micky and that year, the opportunity came to perform in the Big Value Comedy Show. The Big Value Comedy Shows are an established showcase of the best new talent on the comedy circuit and are presented every year at The Edinburgh Festival Fringe. The acts are selected and produced by 'Just the Tonic' Darrell Martin and Joe Dickens and the likes of Sarah Millican, Stephen K Amos, Jason Manford, Jon Richardson, Seann Walsh and Josie Long are some of the famous comics who were first spotted by Big Value.

The Edinburgh Festival Fringe is the largest arts festival in the world and takes place every August for the entire month in Scotland's capital city. There are thousands of comic hopefuls hoping to get 'spotted' and get a 'big break', who come to Edinburgh to perform on one of the multitude of stages all over the city. The Big Value Comedy Shows, which launched in the same year Micky decided to take his comedy course, were to give him a bit of a confidence boost and he took to the stage in the 'Late' show. Comedy promoter Screaming Blue Murder were hosting the evening at the Café Royal and the usual ingredients of three comics, one compere and a run-down venue that served up plenty of beer breaks, seemed like the perfect place to showcase his unique stand-up set. The midweek crowd were very lively that night and compere Greg Burns got them over-excited with the promise of a night of finely packed punchlines. Costing just £6.50 for two hours of comedy, it was one of the most popular nights of the festival and 'Cockney funny man' (as he was billed) Micky went down a treat, as did his fellow acts, Sally Holloway and American cowboy Glenn Wool. It was the kick of confidence that he needed and he started believing that he could do just as well in front of a big crowd as he could at the smaller pubs and clubs across London.

In 2003, he returned to Edinburgh in August to co-headline a show with popular ventriloquist star Nina Conti. The year before, Nina had won the BBC New Comedy Award with her ventriloquist dummies – Granny

and Monk – and she was gaining popularity for her laugh-out-loud unusual acts, coupled with her good looks and unassuming stage presence. It was at the Edinburgh Festival Fringe (EFF) that she and Micky would share centre stage, performing a 'game of two halves' show that would give them 30 minutes in front of a crowd at The Pleasance Courtyard, 'Venue 33'.

Pleasance has two main hubs for performance – The Pleasance Dome on Bristo Square and The Pleasance Courtyard, located on The Pleasance, a street off the Royal Mile. The Pleasance Courtyard at the Edinburgh Festival Fringe was one of the four most prestigious venues, thanks to it being home to the Pleasance Grand, which seats 700 and is one of the largest Fringe venues available. It is also most popular for its comedy acts and attracts the biggest names to perform, ergo the biggest crowds. Micky and Nina would be sharing 30 minutes each in the Attic room of the Pleasance, which seats 58. It is an intimate venue but one that offers a great deal of potential as those who have performed in there during EFFs have gone on to become household names.

Micky was due to appear after Nina's set and the idea of two acts sharing the 60-minute slot was because neither comic could hold their own in front of an audience for the full hour. But the crowd disagreed; and most of the reviews of the show were keen to point out that Micky had great potential and didn't deserve to 'share' a slot. 'Micky Flanagan delivers 30 minutes of acceptable stand-

up but I want to see Micky in his own show, not because he deserves it, but because he doesn't deserve this,' wrote radionewt.org.

'Nina Conti's smart, slightly postmodern ventriloquism is a joy,' wrote the website www.cix.co.uk, 'But her comedic partner this year Micky Flanagan renders it a show of two halves. Three stars.'

The Scotsman wrote: 'It's difficult to decide whether this game of two halves format is a good thing or not. On the one hand, you get twice as many laughs for your money but on the other, there is always a vague suspicion that neither performer is strong enough to sustain an hour-long show on their own. Which is a shame because both Nina Conti and Micky Flanagan are pretty good at what they do.'

But *The Stage*, a prominent magazine in the entertainment industry, didn't think Micky was quite up to scratch just yet.

'Micky Flanagan is in serious need of something startling and new-pin-like to buck up an ailing set. There's a lot which is amiable about his material,' they wrote, 'but he is too young to be doing observational old-man routines about slippers and nodding off in clubs. Yes, there is the odd chortle but it lacks serious guffaws.'

This wasn't to be the last time Micky and Nina worked together and they performed again on 17 October, this time on more familiar territory for Micky, in London at the Soho Theatre.

By now he had begun to really hone his set, deciding that his upbringing in the East End was the ideal material to adapt and use for his stand-up. It was, of course, a subject he could embellish and joke about all he liked; he had lived it, and in hindsight, the experiences he had were perfect to regale an audience. He had put together a set that the crowd could relate to and showed himself as a normal fella, moving out of his East End working-class background to become a 'middle-class ponce' as he puts it.

Performing at the Soho Theatre on that chilly October evening was a big thrill for Micky. At the heart of the comedy scene in Soho, it is home to a 150-seater theatre as well as a 90-seat venue, Soho Upstairs.

The evening was a success and although the *Evening Standard* observed that neither act was quite ready for its own full-hour billing, there was great potential ahead.

'A pair of acts with no discernible connection except that they are both at that awkward stage – too big for 20 minute club sets, too small to sustain an entire hour. A doubleheader is the perfect showcase. Micky charts his life as a game of two halves. After umpteen menial jobs, this genial East Ender gained a degree and suddenly became bourgeois. His observations across the cultural divide, such as the fact that you can spot a middle-class dinner party because the telly is off, are hardly *Das Kapital* but easily digestible.'

This was an important time for Micky, the need to keep

plugging away at his craft was crucial, but that wasn't to say he didn't enjoy the odd bit of down time that came with being a stand-up comedian.

'Since childhood I have enjoyed doing proper f**k all on a regular basis. I would not last long on *The Apprentice*,' he told ComedyCentral website in 2010. 'Apart from me, who is the hardest working comedian? Don't make me laugh, most comics have not got a hard day's work in them!'

Micky, who was used to working from the crack of dawn at the fish market or being in a physically demanding job, such as making furniture or painting and decorating, was certainly finding the slower pace of being a comedian an unusual, if not wonderful, way of life. But his mum and dad were still trying to get their heads around the fact that their son's latest career move was as a comic. Whether it was his past history of not sticking to something for very long or the fact that they couldn't understand why people thought their son was funny, Jim and Sylvie were as blunt as ever when years later, Micky spoke to them about the days he started in comedy. In the extra sections of his Out Out DVD, he held a conversation with his parents about the first time they discovered he would be entering the world of comedy and his mum was perfectly blunt in her answer – it was the 'biggest surprise of her life!' she told him.

His dad was equally honest about how he remembered feeling, the day his son announced he was going to be a comedian.

'I'm a gambling man, I love a bet, as you know,' Jim told Micky. 'But if someone had said to me you were going to be a comic, I would have said no way in the world. I would not have gone for that bet, not even at 100-1!'

Micky and his parents shared quite an open discussion about his decision to be a comic and Jim even revealed that he still had a place at Billingsgate on stand-by if it all went horribly wrong.

'I've often wondered what made you decide to do it,' confessed his mum. 'How did you come to think, "I could do that, I want to do that." And don't they always buy their mums a new house when they're famous?'

'You know you can always come back down the market, all is forgiven!' chipped in his dad (Out Out DVD).

Even though the conversation was shrouded in sarcasm, the underlying feeling that both parents were very proud of Micky is evident. And they were about to be prouder still when, over the next couple of years, he took on two new roles – that of being a husband and a father.

Chapter 5

MEET THE TROUBLE AND STRIFE

'It's OK to say to an audience, "I've read a lot of books, I've got an education." I don't hide the facts like having a wife who is completely your equal. If not your superior. But I've got more money! Ha ha!'

INDEPENDENT, 2011

October 2004 saw Micky head to Brighton to perform with Julian Clary at the Dome. It was the day after he turned forty-two and he told the audience that he was feeling distinctly middle-aged. The show, which was introduced by Julian Clary, was part of the Laughter for Life Comedy Central programmes and the audience warmed to his jokes – they remained rooted in his experiences as a middle-aged man now living in 'middle-class suburbia'. There were plenty of jokes about being a young 'player' and how he 'pulled women' and

got them to sleep with him by whipping out the dragon kimono. It was a gag that always got a lot of laughs when he brought it out and he enjoyed retelling how in the eighties he would wine and dine his dates with a Steak Diane and a Cinzano. There were, as yet, no jokes about a 'trouble and strife' or wife but that was about to change.

With his education behind him now and having gone from reading the *Mirror* to 'the big paper', Micky firmly classed himself as 'middle class' and as such, started dating a 'different kind of woman'.

'They were independent, had strong opinions, smart, intelligent, demanding women,' he told an audience in 2010.

Catherine (Cathy) Lester was one such woman. Working for the English National Opera Company when they met, she was very passionate about art and culture, having earned herself a degree at the prestigious Chelsea School of Art. One evening in 2000, she was persuaded to visit a comedy club, where Micky was performing, by some of her friends.

After the show, Micky went upstairs to the bar and got chatting to her, assuming she had seen the show. But it was only when someone came up to congratulate him on his set and she asked why that he revealed that he had done a comedy gig downstairs. She then admitted she had spent the whole of Micky's set upstairs drinking in the bar and didn't have a clue that he was a budding comedian. 'That

ruins my chances of sleeping with you, dunnit?' Micky exclaimed. 'I don't know about that...' Cathy retorted.

From that moment on, Micky's player days were over. They had met on neutral ground and now Cathy knew about his aspirations to be a comic she started coming to watch some of his gigs as they dated. Their first date was a memorable occasion for them both as Cath agreed to go on a date with Micky but only if she could watch a Mark-Anthony Turnage opera that was coming to the end of its run at the London Coliseum. The opera, *The Silver Tassie*, which is set in during the First World War in a town in Britain, is split into four acts. It didn't appeal to Micky in the slightest – he was planning on taking her for a meal at Nando's restaurant as a new one had just opened on the Bethnal Green Road – but in the pursuit of true love, he put on his smartest shirt and jacket, and picked up Cathy to take her to the opera. She knew that he hated every minute of it but she was touched that he sat through it without complaint (at over two hours long, this was a big achievement for him).

The first date might not have been a success for Micky (although he later revealed that he was just grateful he didn't have to pay for the show) but the following courtship was. Both being in their late thirties, early forties, they soon knew they were in a long-term relationship and marriage was more than likely on the cards and so they bought a house together in East Dulwich.

There is a heartfelt exchange between Micky and Cathy

when they chat about their early dates in a recording for his Radio 4 show, *What Chance Change?* They are both in the 'over-priced' kitchen of their East Dulwich home and Micky introduces her as his 'beautiful' wife. She recalls that he wanted to take her to Nando's for their first date.

'Oh, the glamour!' she told listeners. 'When we met I was working for the National Opera Company and there had been a run of a new Mark-Anthony Turnage opera and it was the last evening and I hadn't seen the whole production, so I said to Mick, we could go out but he'd have to come with me to the opera. He was all suited and booted when he picked me up; he had a smart jacket on, too. I had thrown him in at the deep end and I could feel him grimacing next to me.'

Micky recalled that his biggest problem about watching the opera was that he wasn't allowed to giggle during the performance: 'It was hard work cos you're not allowed to laugh, are you? When people are singing about domestic violence, I don't know how you can't laugh. You know that bit when he was singing, "beating her, beaaat-ing her". I had to sit there and take it seriously. I just wanted to laugh and I wanted to ask the audience, why aren't you laughing? Are you all watching the same thing as me? This man is singing about beating his wife... when was this a good idea?'

It wasn't only the opera that Micky and Cathy would find themselves disagreeing on either, but far from being embarrassed that he didn't like the theatre or art galleries

or museums, Cathy gave him the confidence to be openly dismissive and not hide his feelings about certain things.

He told the *Independent* in 2011: 'Museums and art… I find them so uninteresting and boring. I don't have that middle-class desire to consume culture. I'm not ashamed of it. I don't feel under peer-pressure to say, "I went to that gallery, it was superb." I'm quite happy to go to it but come back and say, "It was boring."'

They had only been dating for a year when they started living together in 2001 and Micky had already warned his girlfriend that as a stand-up he would be out most Thursday, Friday, Saturday and Sunday evenings, doing gigs. That was fine – Cathy accepted the situation and was used to him working unsociable hours. But Micky also warned her that on a Monday night he would often see 'the boys', going to the pub with his mates. This wasn't an issue until one memorable Monday evening when he had gone out with the boys but had also told her he would bring back a bottle of wine and a takeaway. The following story, which he later used in his Back in the Game tour, recalls that he got completely drunk and didn't end up coming home until 1am. The next morning, when he thought he would be in the doghouse for days and knew he had a lot of making up to do, the Twin Towers were the target of a terrorist attack and the world watched in horror as two planes were deliberately flown into the New York skyscrapers. Micky was shocked by the tragedy but he tells the tale that although upset by the attack, he

knew immediately he'd be off the hook from his night of boozing. He told Cathy it put everything in perspective – and it worked.

When he told this tale on his second tour, it got a mixed reaction from the crowd. Some of them laughed as in 'I can't believe he's talking about 9/11 in that way' while others were adamant that it was unnecessary – Micky wasn't a sensational or risqué comic who enjoyed shocking the audience with outrageous stories, like Frankie Boyle, for example, and this didn't sit right with the rest of his set. *Time Out* magazine wrote: 'Very funny, very rude, very honest, 98% pure genius but the 9/11 joke – bin it mate, you're better than that.'

The important part of this particular story, of course, is that they remained a couple and carried on living together happily for years. In 2006, while Cathy was working at the Victoria and Albert Museum (V&A), the world's largest museum of decorative arts that houses a collection of over 4.5 million objects and was named after Queen Victoria and Prince Albert, and Micky was just a few years away from becoming a household name, they decided to get married. It was a simple but beautiful ceremony and it wasn't long before Cathy fell pregnant. Their son Max was born in the same year and the event was one of the greatest days of Micky's life – not to mention his parents, who were proud that their son had finally seemed to settle into something at last – parenthood!

When Max was six months old, like many new mums

Cathy decided she needed to return to work to regain some of her former identity and Micky took on house-husband duties. It suited him to look after Max while working on his stand-up shows and then in the evenings, he would continue to perform at a few open-mic spots. It was a situation that he would later refer to in his stand-up routines and he frequently made reference to his wife and their daily habits as part of his Back in the Game tour. But not, he says, without Cathy's consent. The references he makes to his wife in live shows and when being interviewed are almost always about them being from different social backgrounds and their differences in day-to-day activities. In particular, Micky would have the audience in stitches in describing how she would love to spend the day multi-tasking while he would relish doing 'sod all. Proper sod all' (Out Out tour). This part of his act is always popular and Micky then describes life as a married couple who decide they would like to start a family. Although according to him it is his wife who wants to do so and when they have a child, he tells the audience, he takes over the chief childcare role after six months as Cathy wants to go back to work.

He then sets up the gag about being in a supermarket with his child and having a blokish stand-off with another dad and a pushchair. It struck a chord with men in the audience of his Out Out gigs when he described the situation at the shops.

'I resented the £500 pram initially, then I got involved

in a race in Somerfields. Some dickhead in some fold-up buggy tried to cut me up. I said f**k off mate, there's a monkey's worth of pramette coming through here. It's lovely having a baby, it really is.'

Family life suited Micky down to the ground while also giving him lots of material to later use for his shows about getting older, becoming middle class and dealing with the small, exciting things in life – like when his wife leaves him for the day and he can enjoy doing 'proper f**k all'.

Cath wasn't a brilliant cook. 'Put it this way, she's a career girl,' admitted Micky affectionately, when asked who was the chef of the Flanagan household in an interview with the *Radio Times* in 2012. And they don't always agree on what TV to watch either: Micky isn't keen on her love of period dramas, while Cath's equally unenthused over his choice of programme.

'I just hate everything about period dramas: the self-importance, the ridiculous stories, the low-level luridness – like a bad Carry On film without the jokes. I'm a real fan of things like *The Planet's Funniest Animals*. Dog on a skateboard: Is there anything funnier? I will watch those and my wife comes in and goes, "What on earth are you doing? I've ended up with a mad person." Because if I put her in front of a show like that, she would just go, "This is half an hour of my life I'm not going to get back. I don't want to see a parrot walking along with a hat on." And I'll just go, "Why not? A parrot dressed as a pirate? That's funny!" I also like Harry Hill's *TV Burp*. It's one

of the few programmes where I'm guaranteed to get one or two really good laughs. A good laugh every 12 minutes is a fantastic ratio in TV. And *Deal or No Deal* is my guilty pleasure too. I see that as a little treat to myself: if I get a couple of hours' writing done, I make a cup of tea and watch Noel tell people about "life-changing" money. Now, Noel, £16,000 is barely going to get you a new bathroom in London.'

But like any good 'support act' it is his wife that he talks about most in the show, the person he runs most of his jokes past before he tries them out on even the smallest audience and the person he goes to to help get him in the mood to entertain.

'I like to get myself in the mood to be funny by acting immature and talking bollocks to anyone that'll listen. My wife often has to endure this process. During a recent, particularly dramatic episode of *Lark Rise to Candleford*, I asked her if she thought they were into anal sex during that period. No response. "Good-morrow," I said, and duly went on my way.' (Out Out tour).

It was quite ironic that Micky confessed to being a fan of Harry Hill's *TV Burp* as when the show ended in 2012, it was comedian Harry himself who told *Heat Magazine* in an interview that the only person he could see taking over the show would be someone like Micky.

'I do miss *TV Burp*, I was hoping that someone else would take over,' Harry told the celebrity magazine. 'I was talking to Micky Flanagan and I was hoping he would do

it. It's a lot of work though. I'm the only mug that would do it.'

Having a son put Micky's life into perspective and as someone who felt he was very much let down by his education as a youngster, he made sure that Max was going to get the best possible start in life that he could – and he would certainly encourage him into higher education at every opportunity. It was a topic that Micky felt very strongly about and one that he was happy to elaborate on to the listeners of his Radio 4 show, *What Chance Change?*

'I've had to find a partner who believes in those values too as when the subject of getting an education comes up and some people tell me, "Oh, it doesn't matter if he [Max] doesn't go to university," I always think, actually yes, it does. I was a very angry young man, thinking back at my school life, so these things are important.'

Micky and Cathy decided to enrol Max into a Montessori school which approaches education in a holistic way. He mentions this in his Out Out shows. The approach is that children learn best by doing and that 'happy, self-motivated learners form positive images of themselves as confident, successful people. Dr Maria Montessori aims to develop the whole child and fundamental to the approach is the belief that a child's early years from birth to six are the period when they have the greatest capacity to learn,' according to the www.montessori.org website.

Now Micky had his personal life on track, it was time

to try and hit the big time professionally, and 2007 was going to be the year when he did just that. At the beginning of the year he continued to visit the comedy clubs around London and in February he performed at the Banana Cabaret in Balham. The Banana Cabaret has a worldwide reputation among comics and audiences alike and has seen some of the very best comedians take to the stage in the vast Shakespearean Globe Theatre and ballroom. Micky would be following in the footsteps of Harry Hill, Al Murray, Jack Dee, Will Smith, Frank Skinner and Omid Djalili, to name but a few. The *Surrey Comet* observed that although he 'instantly satisfied the cockney stereotype' by turning up for the interview straight from a pie and mash shop in Bethnal Green, they nevertheless loved the fact that his act did not rely upon stereotypical Cockney behaviour – 'His experiences naturally inform his critically-acclaimed comedy act, which should help him shake off preconceptions of being just another cheeky, chirpy, cockney geezer.'

But 2007 wasn't just to be another run of small-time pubs and comedy clubs for Micky, this was the year he was about to take his first full-length comedy show to the acclaimed Edinburgh Festival Fringe. And then the fun really started...

Chapter 6

A BOTTLE OF RED SAUCE, PLEASE

'I was 33 when I started comedy. The confidence level of those who have worked and those who haven't is very obvious. Those who haven't done an honest job in their lives are far more confident. They know no different. And the ones who have worked can't believe what they are doing, they expect someone to come and say, "OK, OK, time to give it a rest now, you've had a go..."'

WHAT CHANCE CHANGE? RADIO 4 SHOW

Micky stood waiting at the side of the stage for his call to go on. He was dressed in his now usual show attire – a dark shirt and dark trousers, with his curly black hair smart enough not to distract the audience while slightly wild enough to show that he's still a blokey bloke who doesn't do 'preening'.

He was nervous, there was no doubting that but after

nearly 10 years of doing stand-up comedy gigs in smaller pubs and clubs here he was, at Pleasance Courtyard Cellar at the Edinburgh Festival Fringe, ready to present his very first full-length show. He had his set of gags all ready to deliver and he knew they would be good – they had worked to smaller audiences before, there was no reason why they wouldn't work now.

Ricky Gervais was also in the Scottish capital, charging £37.50 for fans to watch him perform 90 minutes of stand-up at the Edinburgh Castle, Castle Hill, while Josie Long and Jon Richardson would also be among some of the more well-known comics taking to the stage for the month of August to entertain the crowds. Over the next few weeks that is just what Micky would be doing. There was no half hour to fill now, no act to share the slot with; it was time for Micky alone to take to the stage for the full 60 minutes and entertain. It was 1 August 2007 and there was a small audiences waiting for him to do just that on a rainy Wednesday evening.

Nine months earlier, at the end of 2006, he had decided that it was time for him to tackle his own show at the Edinburgh Fringe. The half-and-half shows he had shared with Nina Conti had gone down well and his confidence had increased with several well-received gigs since then. Plus, with a new wife and baby, he was unstoppable. Spending the last few months of 2006 looking after his newborn son while his wife went back to work allowed him (alongside child-rearing duties, of

course) to work on his act, writing and re-writing gags that he knew worked in front of an audience but needed a little tweaking.

'You come up with a story first, and if the story has a nice rhythm to it, and you've got a nice ending to it, then your job is to also try and put other jokes in there,' he told GQ *Magazine* in 2013. 'And they're always there; sometimes they just take rewrites and rewrites but the story essentially starts and ends in the same place, but if you can get three more laughs in there, now you've got a great story.'

The act, entitled, 'What Chance Change?' was to define his comedy career as it gave the audience a chance to know the real Micky. His one-man case study in social mobility – of rising from Billingsgate fish porter to 'full-blown middle-class ponce' as he so eloquently put it, means that his work appeals to most people. Some of his jokes in the set were a little rude but there was no need for Micky to censor his routine at this stage – he wasn't performing a family-friendly set on the BBC just yet. This was for fans of comedy who wanted to belly-laugh their way through a night that was risqué, cheeky and took them back to the years when being PC wasn't necessary and class was much more defined.

His now infamous joke about asking for ketchup in a posh French restaurant was getting its first big-time outing, having received applause in all the pubs in which he had previously performed it. It is one of my personal favourites

and Micky tells it brilliantly – when embarrassing his wife by asking for ketchup (or rather tomato sauce), the waitress delivers a small white dish of it to his table before Micky takes a sip and, finding the taste agreeable, asks for the bottle. It is a gag that will be told to perfection time and time again, later on his Out Out tours too, and sums up Micky's life quite perfectly – you can take the working-class man out to a middle-class restaurant but you can't take the working-class out of the man in the middle-class restaurant.

Micky was understandably excited about his time in Edinburgh for the festival, having built himself up to it during the previous nine months. In a commentary that he wrote for the *Observer* in 2010 about his first time performing solo, he gave a personal account of how he felt, taking to the stage in a city that was expecting big laughs from an as-yet unknown performer. But he was ready to be discovered.

I'm driving into the city in a taxi and there's no turning back. I'm one of thousands of performers using hundreds of venues with one goal: get an audience and get discovered. The first night looms and I feel equal amounts of fear and excitement. To be at their best, stand-ups have to be nervous but not scared, rehearsed but not wooden, want the audience to like them but not care if they don't. I am ready. I think.

With my head down I walk across North Bridge, where panpipes are competing with bagpipes, and I'm so focused I don't look up at the castle. I glance into Pizza Hut where I sat 10 years ago just before I was about to do my heat of 'So You Think You're Funny'. Brand new to the world of stand-up, I didn't have a clue how important this city became for a month every year. A city where people get discovered and discarded in equal measure, a place where you can see mind-blowing talent and utter shite in rapid succession. Where you can follow the five-star reviews and be totally disappointed or take a punt on some maniac who's lying down in the Royal Mile and faking a fit before handing out flyers to people who go to his aid. You'll tell your friends, 'You gotta see Epileptic Boy on at 3.30pm in the public toilets on Leith Walk. He actually rolls around in the piss while reading *Plato's Republic*. Genius!'

On stage and things are going well with almost a full house. A stiff local audience give me the once-over. An old man with a hill-walking stick looks like he's wishing he'd gone for a stroll. A smile turns to a chuckle and he's on board. I never really get them all but the show goes well for a first night. Sitting backstage, I'm thinking about it too much. My friend Claire pokes her head around the door. 'Pint?' she says. Now... is there anyone important in the bar?'

Micky's very personal account shows exactly how much the show meant to him. It was his first proper chance to make it into the big time and he was conscious of giving a well-rehearsed show that didn't make him look stiff or wooden. His analysis of his first night performance meant he made tweaks to some parts of his act in the subsequent nights, performing until the end of the month, 26 August, at the same venue.

To say that the audiences and critics were impressed is an understatement. Chortle (www.chortle.co.uk) stated that although 'it is a belated Edinburgh debut for 44 year-old Flanagan, he is one of the more enjoyable, personable and cheerful acts on the circuit.'

They went on to praise him as a comedy performer and praise one of his gags as 'one of the funniest routines in the festival, especially the one about asking for ketchup in posh restaurants which is not only hilarious, but fits in beautifully with his theme of being stuck between classes. There are lots of proper jokes in "What Chance Change?" In fact, it's built entirely on the most efficient way of getting from one to the next.'

The List (www.edinburghfestival.list.co.uk) was equally impressed. In its review of 9 August, they praised Micky's ability to cut it in a young man's world in making his festival debut at the ripe old age of forty-four.

Stand-up at the Fringe might be viewed by some as a young person's game but there is surely room for

the more senior of our comedy talents to shuffle on to Edinburgh's stages. At the tender age of 44, Micky Flanagan isn't ready for his Zimmer frame just yet but he has chosen this moment to make his Festival debut. He has welded his varied life experiences to produce a show entitled 'What Chance Change?' And the anecdotes ripple out to an audience being happily seduced by his jovial metropolitan ways and old school sex talk. Flanagan is in possession of a gentle set, leaving all that breakneck delivery and concept show stuff to the young ones. Skipping from one amusing story to another, the hour takes on little shape with nothing solid to truly connect this flow.

It was a positive start and Micky would take on board what was said and would later perfect the running of his gags with storytelling in between to link them seamlessly. The reviews were positive, the audience loved his nightly routines but the icing on the cake was still to come. On 22 August, the nominations were announced for the 2007 IF Comedy Awards (now renamed the Edinburgh Comedy Awards or 'Eddies') and Micky was nominated in the Best Newcomer category.

The Stage announced that 'The Newcomer's shortlist was hotly contested with a number of promising first-time solo shows.' Micky was up against Jon Richardson, Tom Basden and Zoe Lyons, with the awards ceremony taking place on 25 August. To be even nominated was a

fantastic achievement for him, proving that after 10 years of perfecting his craft, he could hold his own amongst the bigger comedy giants. He didn't win, the award went to Tom Basden for his show, *Tom Basden Won't Say Anything*, but it didn't matter. He had made his mark and now critics, fellow comedians and audiences were starting to take note.

'The rising star,' was the opinion of Stephen Armstrong of *The Sunday Times*. 'If there was any justice in the world he'd be a huge star,' wrote Tim Arthur of *Time Out* magazine. 'The future of comedy,' confirmed Frank Skinner.

It was a tremendous reaction to his show and now Micky had made his mark, he was determined not to rest on his laurels.

He decided to take his 'What Chance Change?' show to the Soho Theatre and from 17 to 19 January 2008, at 8pm, performed for a packed theatre. It was another success.

William Cook noted in the *Guardian*:

There's nothing quite so irritating as a mockney stand-up comic, but unlike most comedians with estuary accents, Micky Flanagan is the genuine article. And while well-bred comics strangle their vowels in a desperate bid to sound hip and streetwise, this cockney comic has spent 25 years travelling in the opposite direction. In 1980 he was living in the

East End and working as a fish porter in London's Billingsgate market and now he's living in demure East Dulwich and a comedian. It's a job he's been doing for 10 years now and he's really very good at it. Unlike a lot of younger, posher stand-ups, he's lived enough to know who he really is and he hasn't spent his life in a cosy ghetto, cocooned by people who all think the same way. Along the way he's done a degree and traded in street parties for dinner parties. This one-man show describes the journey.

By the end of 2007 Micky had also been approached by the BBC to take part in their new Radio 2 series, *Out to Lunch*, scheduled to air in the spring of the following year. It was a series that was first broadcast in 2006, with Russell Howard and Rob Deering, and by the time Micky joined in May 2008, Russell Kane had taken over hosting duties and was joined each week by comics Dan Antopolski, Micky, Colin & Fergus and a different special guest for an hour of stand-up, sketches and character monologues.

As well as performances at the Soho Theatre and becoming a regular on Radio 2, he was one of only a handful of comics to perform their own Comedy Central special.

It wasn't long before Micky was being booked every night of the week and it was time that he got himself an agent to represent him for future, more big-time bookings.

Christian Knowles Productions (CKP) was the company to do just that, an agency that had been in the comedy industry for over 15 years. They had worked with some established household names – including radio breakfast show host Christian O'Connell – as well as upcoming, emerging comedy talents. Christian Knowles himself became Micky's agent and if 2007 was to be the year he first tasted the mouth-watering *amuse-bouche* of fame, 2009 was when he well and truly devoured the main course. It was a year that would make him a household name and by the end of it, he'd have a UK-wide tour lined up and ready to go...

But 2009 started off fairly modestly. Micky was now performing his own hour-long sets in bigger venues and in January he appeared in the Leicester Comedy Festival Preview Show, an event not often frequented by die-hard stand-up fans, therefore offering the performers a chance to work their gags in front of a perhaps less easily impressed bunch. That didn't make it any less of an event, however: there was a sell-out crowd of over 1,700 and Micky was one of the highlights of the night, according to Chortle's website.

'The other highlight of the night was the far more conventional Micky Flanagan, regaling us with his stories of being a working class Cockney Herbert made good. He is, literally, a class act. This is social commentary many can relate to but deftly delivered as personal anecdotes,' they wrote. 'The breezy Flanagan has charm by the sack-

full and a finely honed talent for benevolent piss-taking, with himself more often than not, the victim of his good-natured joshing.' (www.chortle.co.uk)

January wasn't all about face-to-face performances, though, Micky was set to bring his very own radio show to the airwaves and on Tuesday, 6 January at 11pm, he took listeners of Radio 4 on a journey through his past to what made him the comic he is today. It was an abbreviated set but still called, 'What Chance Change?' The listeners loved it and the radio bosses decided to commission him to perform his own series of the show the following year, each week depicting a different decade that had shaped him – from school life to working life. Over the four weeks he introduced the listeners to members of his family (a different family member introduced the show each week and in the final week, his son Max welcomed his 'daddy' to the show) and took listeners through his life. There were interludes of stand-up footage and Micky discussed certain aspects of his life with various people that played an important part in it – the mates he went to school with, a university tutor, and comedian Sean Lock, with whom he discussed being a comedian of a certain age.

In March, Micky performed his set to the Just For Laughs Montreal Festival Showcase at the London Comedy Store. It was more than just a regular gig, comedians were performing in front of talent scouts from the Montreal Festival, a crowd of comedy industry people that shows like this invariably attract and of course,

the punters themselves. And Micky didn't disappoint. Coming last to the stage to finish off the evening, even though the running order was drawn at random, it was noted that, 'You probably couldn't do better than have the increasingly impressive Micky Flanagan headline the show. A fine end to a packed night.'

While that might have been pretty exhausting for a man who had been just performing at small venues the past 10 years, this was the chance he had been waiting for and he certainly wasn't afraid of a little hard work.

'The pitfall of doing this job professionally is to not take it seriously,' he said in an interview with website entertainment.ie in 2012. 'To get the impression that it is just a laugh is a mistake. It's a job you have to take very seriously if you want to move forward. That means behaving like a professional, getting to the show on time and being a very responsible performer. All the things you can control. Get there on time and be polite to the promoter, don't cause a fuss or upset the customers. All of those things and then try and be as funny as possible.'

His job was one he took very seriously indeed and with the big time beckoning, Micky was ready to appeal to a more family-friendly audience. How was he going to succeed in doing that? Well, it was all thanks to another comedian called Michael...

Chapter 7

TIME TO GO OUT, OUT

'You know what I mean by "out out", don't ya? You "pop out" to go to the shops, get milk and a cut loaf and you see a friend who invites you for a quick drink. Three hours later, you're still in the pub, you're now "out". And then the evening people come in and these people are going out properly. What we like to call, "out out". They ask if you want to come out with them and you say, I can't come "out out". I wasn't even meant to be coming out.'

OUT OUT TOUR

Thirty-eight-year-old Michael McIntyre is reportedly one of the highest-grossing comedians in the world and as well as releasing three DVDs and presenting stints on Comic Relief, he was also a judge on *Britain's Got Talent* in 2011, alongside Amanda Holden and David

Hasselhoff. He has appeared in countless panel shows, including *Mock The Week*, *8 Out of 10 Cats*, *Have I Got News For You*, *Chris Moyles' Quiz Night* and *The Big Fat Quiz Of The Year*, not to mention performing three times at the Royal Variety Performance and having a record-breaking first UK tour which saw him perform for six nights at Wembley Arena and four at The O2 Arena. At the time of writing he has a BBC1 late-night chat show too.

Following his successful appearances on *Live at the Apollo* (he appeared three times, in 2007, 2008 and 2009), it was announced in February 2009 that Michael would be hosting a new comedy series for BBC entitled *Michael McIntyre's Comedy Roadshow*. The structure of the series was for Michael to visit some of the best comedy venues around the country to take to the stage and perform. He would then be joined by three other comedians – some well-established and some relatively new – as they performed their acts before the programme closed with a headline act.

It was an exciting prospect as the show would air on the BBC in a Saturday night prime-time slot, giving those comedians who performed the chance to reach out to a nationwide audience. They would be on telly, telling their jokes to millions of people across the country, not to mention in front of a packed live audience. In April the line-ups for the shows were announced and in episode six, the final episode of the series, Michael McIntyre would

be heading to Brighton to perform at the Dome. He'd be joined on stage by headline act Al Murray, plus Jo Caulfield, Jon Richardson and Micky Flanagan. This was it: Micky would be hitting a whole new level of fame that was to change his life, and he was ready. He had performed in front of large crowds before but this would be different. Now he was in a line-up for a BBC comedy show and he didn't want to disappoint. Not that that was ever going to happen but with limited time on stage (it was a 45-minute show and he had just under 10 minutes to fill), he had to pick his gags carefully. He knew that he had a good crop to pick from, years of honing his set meant that he had a repertoire of useable gags but the family-friendly BBC also didn't want some of his more risqué material making it on air, worried it might cause complaints and upset the viewers at home. Micky, although slightly put out, wasn't overly perturbed.

'TV is kind when it comes to putting bums on seats,' he observed in an interview with the *Independent* a few years later. 'I've had to play the game. You get the opportunity to go on Michael McIntyre's *Comedy Roadshow* and five minutes before you go on they say, "You can't do that bit." So you go out and do a nice 10 minutes of TV-friendly comedy.'

Micky knew what gags would be making the cut, though, and when Michael welcomed him on to the stage, he was ready to showcase his talents. Dressed in a metallic dark silver long-sleeved shirt and black trousers, he took

to the stage with his microphone and gave it his best shot. Starting with his background gag about growing up in the East End, being in a school with the only kid who had ambition – Gary Hutton, cos he wanted to drive a van – he then told the audience how he was finding being a middle-aged, middle-class man and how he hated queuing up outside a nightclub but loved being turned away by the bouncer because he's so tired. And of course, there was his gag about asking for tomato sauce in the posh restaurant. He saved that until last, knowing it would get the most laughs (which of course, it did).

Micky also performed his now infamous Out Out routine, about the way British people have different levels of drunkenness on a night out (see sketch above).

It was seven minutes of comedy gold and the audience loved it. Viewers at home couldn't get enough of it, either. He performed it to perfection – after years of practising it in the smaller bars and pubs – and his three-minute Out Out routine was one of the most watched clips on YouTube following the show.

'When I first did it [the Out Out sketch], it got a massive laugh,' he later told the *Daily Telegraph*. 'I went away with a note on my pad saying, "This is going to be good." It became the thing that everyone knew me by, a calling card if you like, my version of Bruce Forsyth's "Nice to see you, to see you, nice."'

They say imitation is the sincerest form of flattery but a few months after performing his Out Out sketch on

the BBC, Micky lodged a complaint with the Advertising Standards Agency that telephone directory enquiry company 118 118 had used his routine in one of its TV campaigns.

'Ever since I started going out drinking it's always been an expression, whether you're going "out" or going "out out", so it's not like I invented it but I picked it up, put it in a routine and got laughs accordingly,' Micky told the website www.Londonisfunny.co.uk. 'I brought it back for the Michael McIntyre show because I knew it was strong and catchy and the BBC put it on YouTube afterwards for promotion. Then suddenly it's on the telly in this advert.'

His agent, Christian Knowles, has accused the company of taking Micky's signature catchphrase and skit for use in its TV adverts. The animated commercial features the phrase 'out out' as a punchline for its campaign and also sets the advert in a nightclub – a measure of Micky's level of being 'out out'.

'I have watched the 118 118 and Micky's clip on YouTube back to back umpteen times and I genuinely believe they have taken it and lifted it,' said Christian. 'Micky has spent years building his career and had only now started to get major recognition, we have to make a stand.'

The ASA acknowledged Christian's complaint that the 'advert clearly mimics your client's idea' but they were unable to take any further action as it was beyond

their remit. They acknowledged that the phrase had been publicly used by Micky but was not an imitation of Micky himself.

'The key factor in the interpretation of the code rule is that it refers specifically to living people,' confirmed the ASA. 'Although the advert clearly mimics your client's idea, it would appear in this instance that your objections are more to do with intellectual property issues, not the representation of Micky Flanagan as a living person per se.'

'I'm annoyed firstly because they didn't pay for it and money has been made from it and also because I was going to use that phrase in the future for the name of a tour or a DVD. But if people think, oh, he has just got that from the telly, it's hard to change their minds on that. It undermines you as a performer.' Micky thought it best to be cautious, adding later: 'Also, when you're a comic, you have to be a little bit careful about standing up and saying you're the only person in the world who ever thought that because someone will then send you a transcript of a Victorian comic in 1899, going, "You know what it's like, you're out and then you're out out." The complaint was me saying, "All right, you've spotted it and you've used it. We know but we can't claim it." There are very few things that you can claim exclusively for your own. Maybe discovering gravity.'

The furore didn't distract from the fact that Micky's catchphrase was getting talked about and therefore in

turn getting him talked about too. They do say there is no such thing as bad publicity and in Micky's case it was true. While he acknowledges he was not overly ambitious at the start of his comedy career, he soon found that after the Edinburgh Festival, the radio show and now Michael McIntyre's show, he was getting more exposure. And he loved it. But he was careful not to compare his level of fame with comedians who had started on the scene long after him, who had now got their own TV shows.

'I wasn't as ambitious but I never cared how well other people were doing. It was about whether I was happy or not,' he told the *Metro* in 2013. 'You're in trouble if you start judging yourself by what other people around you are doing – it's only for you to decide what you want to do. I wanted to take things further five years ago, so did my first hour-long show at the Edinburgh Festival. It's from there I got the Radio 4 Extra series and a few TV breaks.'

In July, he was also invited onto Arthur Smith's Radio 4 show, *Arthur Smith's Balham Bash*, which is a comedy and music show hosted by Arthur and recorded at his house in Balham. The host turned his home into a little club for each episode and would invite musicians and comics to perform in his kitchen, have stand-up shows in his bedroom and interview unexpected guests in his bathroom. Micky appeared in episode three of the first series in July and sounded thoroughly at home in the medium of radio. The Radio 4 team were impressed

by his guest slot and his previous pilot, *What Chance Change?*, and decided to offer him a four-part series of his own. Also entitled, *What Chance Change?*, the series began on 25 May of the following year and in each weekly show, Micky dissected a decade of his life growing up in the East End. The shows were interspersed with performances from his comedy sets but he also invited friends and family to talk about his life and the way things were in the East End in the 1970s and 80s. Listeners and critics wanted more.

'You might not have heard of Micky Flanagan before but this new comedy series should ensure he becomes a regular – on TV as well as radio. His astute take on social mores and the class system are spot on,' reviewed the *Radio Times*.

'If you can find a gap between football games this week, the last of Micky Flanagan's series *What Chance Change?* is well worth a listen,' wrote the *Guardian*. 'Partly recorded at his standup gigs, partly in conversation with his family and friends, Flanagan has charted his life from Billingsgate fish market to middle-class delis. This week, he chatted to Sean Lock and considered middle age – thankfully managing to swerve *Grumpy Old Men* territory.'

The *Observer* was equally enthusiastic: 'I saw Flanagan's stand-up recently and his riffs on life in the yummy mummy enclave of East Dulwich had the audience roaring. *What Chance Change?* takes that routine's premise – how strange it is for a boy from the markets in the East End to

move up a social class – and expands on it. It's excellent, funny and poignant, though you can't help feeling that Radio 4's traditional audience is not quite who Micky is aiming to inspire.'

Meanwhile, Micky continued to work steadily on the circuit, playing bigger theatres and revisiting previous venues that had welcomed him when he first appeared on the scene. In August he went back to the Edinburgh Festival Fringe to perform every night at 8.40pm, from 5–30 August, and was advertised in the programme and on flyers with the caption, 'IF comedy nominee Micky returns for a brand new show'.

Even though it was two years since his last gig there – his first solo performance that earned him the 'Best Newcomer' nomination – the people at the EFF were ready to welcome him back. It wasn't just his confidence on stage that had grown, his fan base had increased, too.

His new stage show, entitled 'Spiel', still incorporated elements of his 'What Chance Change?' gig, but there was a wealth of new material in there, too. He had started doing gags about how he had transmuted from punk rocker into a middle-aged man who liked a new vest. There were plenty of jokes about how he has a lot less sex these days now he has a baby and how he didn't like to go out much any more as he didn't like to miss *Property Ladder* or *Antiques Roadshow*. The show, held at the Pleasance Courtyard again, concluded with his now rather anticipated 'asking for red sauce in a fancy French

restaurant' joke from the original 2007 show and one reviewer, from chortle.co.uk, was a little under-whelmed by the lack of new material.

> He [Micky] tells everything with a cheerful lack of pretension, and a self-deprecating willingness to admit he's often embarrassed by the gaps in his knowledge or middle-aged va-va-voom. But for at least half of 'Spiel', he seems like he is coasting. The non-committal Fringe programme description should probably be taken as an indication this show never had much of a creative drive beyond an hour of general stand-up. But most tellingly, his concluding routine – the moment the whole hour should build towards – is the ketchup-in-a-restaurant gag that was in the original show. It's very funny but in two years he should surely have produced something else to close on.

But if Micky was worried that all his reviewers would be equally unimpressed, it was soon clear that there was no need to panic. 'Spiel' was a big hit among the festival-goers and critics alike. *Ed Fest* magazine referred to his 2008 absence: 'Parenthood meant that Flanagan was unable to capitalise on his 2007 if.comedy nomination as quickly as he'd have wished and he took last Fringe off. But now the roguish cockney charmer is back and we can't wait!' Other reviewers were just pleased to see him back in action.

The Stage noted that Micky's show was 'one of the funniest spots of the festival.' They wrote: 'His laid-back laconic Cockney tones are infectious and lull you into rambling stories before the punch lines spring out of the blue and catch you unawares. Flanagan effortlessly tops my laugh meter for this festival, on paper it all seems pretty ordinary stuff but when seen from Flanagan's socially-warped viewpoint, even the lowly bath tap has unlimited comic potential.'

The Sunday Times found him 'side-splitting' and the *Guardian* had the show as the Critic's Choice. The *Northern Echo* found his 'funny-bloke-down-the-pub banter instantly engaging; he's self-effacing, down-to-earth and a pleasure to watch. He was well received by an enthusiastic audience and, while he's not breaking any new comedy ground, he's sure to become a more familiar face as his inevitable popularity increases.'

Micky came away from Edinburgh happy: the shows had been a success and his hard work was paying off. For him the experience of now doing his job on a bigger scale was the ultimate success. But there were downsides to the job too – like most comedians on the circuit, he worked unsociable hours and was away from home a lot performing – and the strain on family life was to get worse when he began touring.

'The best thing about being a comedian is getting to do what you enjoy most, and that Sunday night/Monday morning feeling becomes a distant memory. The worst

thing is always being out of sync with most other people,' he explained in a *Time Out* interview in 2010. 'Walking past my local pub on the way to work at weekends and seeing everyone enjoy that Friday night feeling. It soon passes when I remind myself about the Sunday/Monday feeling. Perhaps I feel too much? I should write a song.'

He also found that his health suffered from his newfound career. Previously having always worked in fairly physical jobs – as a fish porter, furniture maker and window cleaner and other jobs – he found that his weight slowly crept up while doing stand-up and although not a terribly vain man, he did admit in a 2011 interview with the *Guardian* that he had started to look at how he could improve his appearance now that he was starting to look his age.

'I started looking my age when I was 44, when my son was born. I always did active jobs before I became a stand-up and I noticed the change. So I take care over my diet – lots of vegetables and salad,' he said. 'It sounds vain but there's not a lot I dislike about my appearance, it's my weight, which increased a few years ago that took getting used to. One day I realised I had to buy a pair of 36in-waist jeans. I've stayed that size, despite doing 50 press-ups and sit-ups every day.'

Micky's middle-aged panic about looking old and putting on weight isn't particularly unusual, but he was trying everything he could to tackle his 'middle-aged spread' by doing his daily exercises and watching what he

ate, which is not just a vanity issue. To be able to perform stand-up nightly and be on stage talking for an hour at a time might not sound that physical but with the long hours, you need to be fairly fit to come out late at night and be full of energy. Especially if your set involves a lot of physical comedy, like Micky's: he shows audiences how an authentic Cockney walks, bustling across the stage backwards and forwards every night.

Micky has a mop of thick black curly hair and heavy-set black eyebrows that make him appear more youthful than he actually is. The name Flanagan suggests perhaps Irish descent but with a family history of Londoners born and bred, there is no Irish blood-line to credit his dark locks to. He reckons there are some Spanish ancestors somewhere in his family that have helped give him his 'Mediterranean look'.

'I'm lucky that I've kept my hair and it's stayed dark,' he told the *Guardian*. 'There's a bit of grey but you have to get close to see it. It adds to my foreign, Mediterranean look. Somewhere down the line, my antecedents are Spanish and if I go there or Greece, I look like a local. And I never burn.'

By the end of 2009 he was back in some of his regular haunts. He saw in 2010 by performing at Banana Cabaret's New Year's Eve party to a very merry, very excitable crowd; the atmosphere was electric and he was loving every minute. Micky wasn't looking to further his career much – being on telly had been the highlight of his

year and career so far – and he was happy continuing life on the circuit.

'I was very happy where I was: being a circuit comic. I didn't have a plan. All I wanted to do was avoid having a badly paid nine-to-five job,' he told the *Portsmouth News* in 2010. There were never going to be any worries about Micky taking a nine-to-five job at the end of 2009, however: the following year was set to bring even more TV exposure, bigger venue shows and also one of the accolades that most comics aspire to, a nationwide tour. Nine-to-five? Ha! Tell us another one, Micky...

LIGHTS, CAMERA, ACTION!

'What is my idea of comedy? Whatever people laugh at.
When you do comedy, you know if it's any good because
people laugh. You can't dissect it all too much. I suppose that
should be the rule for whatever type of comedy you're doing:
if they're laughing, you're doing something right.'

GQ, 2013

The year 2010 began with Micky continuing to take to the stage in comedy clubs, returning to Banana Cabaret in February. Performing on stage was important to him and being a stand-up comic rather than just a comic was the subject of a lively debate – the *Fast Show* comics claimed that panel shows were crowding out other sorts of comedy. Micky could also see a decline in the art

of stand-up and he spoke of how worrying it was that the comedy circuit was 'starting to fragment' in an interview with *GQ Magazine*.

'On the evidence that the club circuit is starting to shrink a little bit, that's worrying. If that carries on, we're going to probably err towards the American model of people wanting to be on TV very quickly so that they can then possibly go on tour themselves. Or to want to appear in sitcoms rather than just be good old fashioned stand-ups. But given that I probably took five years to get established, and that was working on a regular basis, if acts can't do that, how are they going to become really proficient stand-ups? How many years is it going to take them?'

It was an issue that was close to his heart and knowing how hard he had worked at comedy clubs and pubs each night to get himself known, he was cautious about any old venue holding comedy nights for fear of putting off watching stand-up comedy altogether.

'I'd rather have a circuit where everybody's got work on a Friday and Saturday night than a circuit where really good comics haven't. I think what will happen is that the established clubs will carry on doing OK, but it's going to get harder to establish a good old fashioned room above a pub because anyone can start a gig in a pub with a microphone. But if the fifty people who come on that first night don't have a good time, you'll never get them back. Whereas if someone goes to the Comedy Store, the

chances are they'll come away comedy fans,' he told *GQ Magazine* in 2013.

With his radio show, *What Chance Change?*, airing on Radio 4 at the end of May to impressive reviews, Micky was about to make his debut on stage at the Bloomsbury Theatre, a 535-seater venue in London's West End. Micky's show, a culmination of his two Edinburgh Fringe shows, had two dates – Saturday, 8 May and Monday, 24 May – and within hours of the tickets going on sale, both gigs were sold out. It was a testament to how far he had come that he could sell out a 500-plus seater venue in record time, so he took to the stage with confidence, the audience in stitches within minutes.

'Bloody hilarious,' revealed one audience member. 'He needs to go on tour!', while the LondonTown website didn't think it was much of a surprise that the shows were sold out as 'the likeable Flanagan has a firm fan base.' And with fellow comedian Frank Skinner declaring that Micky was 'arguably the funniest comedian in the world,' it was now only a matter of time before that eager fan's desire came true and he took his show around the country...

In June he was offered the chance to travel to India and be one of the comedians that opened the first overseas branch of London's Comedy Store in Mumbai. It was a real honour for Micky and an experience that would later give him plenty of material for future shows too (his Delhi-belly sketches used in his Back in the Game tour, years later, were testament to this). Over 1,000 people

turned up to the event, which saw the 300-seater venue opened by Canadian Craig Campbell, Micky and fellow Brit Paul Tonkinson. It was one of the most exciting yet risky ventures in the career of Don Ward, boss of the London venue.

'In England there are 400 comedy venues, India had none,' he told the BBC Asian Network. 'Now it has one in a city which is home to more than 22 million people. People will see here exactly what you will see in the UK. Every week anyone will be able to come down and take the mic and if they're any good, we'll put them in our shows.'

Micky, Paul and Craig then took it in turns to take to the stage before chatting to some of the locals about being funny. Micky impressed the audience with his gags about leaving school with just a bottle opener and how people in the UK plan when to have sex – fitting it around boiling the rice and watching property renovation shows. The joke that got the most laughs of the night though was about his exercise routines, when he revealed to the audience that he had planned on going to the gym as everyone told him how good it would make him feel. In typical Micky style, he made no bones about the fact that a visit to the gym did indeed make him feel good – but only because he fell asleep on the sit-ups mat!

His experiences in India provided comedy tales that he was subtly storing for future use on stage, but they were also a humbling experience for him. Where he came from,

you could make any joke about anyone without fear. Now The Comedy Store would be home to a raw brand of humour previously unseen in the region and he was proud to be part of it. The local newspapers reported that Micky and his fellow comics were a success and one, the *Hindustan Times*, got a chance to chat to them just after they landed on 12 June.

> The three Comedy Store comics from London crash into the sofa, looking drained and worn out having just landed. Discussing the prospect of performing at the opening of the Comedy Store in Mumbai this weekend, their eyes light up. Flanagan compares the comedian to a musician, where the comic has a 'vague idea' of where the show will go. 'But if something happens on the night, he's happy to follow that tangent. A musician won't. That's part of the enjoyment, the unpredictability of it. You just play with the audience on the night.'

Back in Blighty and Micky found time for a few TV appearances in between his Bloomsbury show and his debut tour announcement. He was on *Mock The Week* on BBC2 on Thursday, 1 July. With Micky joining Dara O'Briain the panel consisted of Hugh Dennis, Russell Howard, Andy Parsons, Chris Addison and Ed Byrne on episode 3 of series 9. Micky was a natural and the studio audience loved him – especially his fancy-restaurant-

asking-for-sauce gag. It was no coincidence perhaps that when Dara spun the wheel for the weekly 'Wheel of News' topics to be debated by the three performers – Micky, Ed and Andy – the first topic up was food, perfect for Micky to take centre stage and deliver the gag. It was still new enough not to be tiresome and it got a roar of applause when he performed the 'yes, I'll have a bottle, please' punchline.

Micky revealed in an interview with the Digital Spy website that you do have to adapt stand-up material for TV shows, though.

'Because of the time limitations on TV, your material inevitably has to get much shorter and tighter and jokier. You literally get seconds, especially on *Mock The Week* where the only chance you get to perform a piece of stand-up is when you're at the "Wheel Of News". Apart from that you better get to the punch line fairly quickly. That's different from my actual stand-up where I like to tell actual stories. I tend to veer towards shorter, punchier bits for panel shows.'

He was back on *Mock The Week* in September and several times the following year, enjoying the one-liners and quick-wit style of the show, as well as the chance to perform little skits. Tim Vine, a fellow comedian, had previously slated the show to entertainment website DigitalSpy, revealing that he couldn't cope with the competitive element of the show, but that didn't bother Micky.

'Comics generally are a one-man band – the only person

you're competing with is yourself and the audience. When you're put in an environment where you've got to be funnier than other people or get to the funny bit a bit quicker than someone else, a lot of comics find it very uncomfortable,' he told the same website. 'Tim made the very grown-up decision of saying it's not for him. I looked at it and thought, "I think I could do that" and gave it a go and found actually it's not as hard as people might make out.'

In fact, TV wasn't as daunting as Micky imagined. Having a couple of *MTW* shows under his belt, the offers started coming in for more TV work for different panel shows. He was approached by Channel 4 to take part in their new series, *Stand Up For The Week*, which saw Patrick Kielty host the Friday evening show live from KOKO club (formerly Camden Palace). Each week Patrick would perform a routine followed by the regular comics – Jack Whitehall, Kevin Bridges, Andi Osho and Rich Hall, and then it would be the turn of the guest comedian. Micky took part in the show in episode 3, which aired on 9 July, helping to discuss topics such as Paris Hilton, the World Cup and some of the strangest web stories hitting the headlines. He was invited back for series 2, which aired on 12 March 2011, and again proved a natural during the filming.

In August it was the annual trip to Edinburgh to take part in the Edinburgh Festival Fringe but this time it wasn't just the die-hard comedy fans who would have the

chance to see Micky in action – he appeared in a sold-out run at the EFF at Pleasance Two, Pleasance Courtyard. The BBC also decided not to miss out on broadcasting some of the funny men and women who were performing to hundreds of fans at the festival and recorded some of the biggest comedy names when they performed at the Festival Theatre in a BBC3 show called *Edinburgh Comedy Fest Live 2010*. Kevin Bridges and Adam Hills hosted the show and Micky took to the stage in the first episode, which aired on Thursday, 2 September. The show also featured routines from Jason Byrne, Stephen K Amos, John Bishop, Justin Moorhouse, Andi Osho, Mark Watson and Andrew Laurence, but Micky brought the house down with his 'chicken children' sketch, about how youngsters today like to congregate by the fried chicken shop.

At the end of the festival there was little time to sit down but Micky did find time to go 'out out' on his last day in Edinburgh before he had to hurry back to London to announce the beginning of his tour.

'Essentially, in Edinburgh on arrival you are out and only a gnat's cock away from being "out out",' he told Comedy Central blog. 'I got on a 6 o'clock train back to London straight from the pub on my last night.'

Back home in London there were a few days' rest at home with Cathy and Max before it was announced that Micky was to embark on his first ever UK tour. Entitled, The Out Out Tour, it was the beginning of an exciting

new chapter in his career. Very soon he'd be playing to hundreds of fans up and down the country in venues of various sizes in a planned 59-show tour. But little did he know when he hit the road to his first venue, the tour would eventually be such a sell-out success, he'd be playing nearly double that many shows…

Chapter 9

TOUR DE FORCE

'The best thing about being on the road? The sense of freedom and being some peripatetic wordsmith spreading joy wherever you go. The worst thing is collecting your things after a show and making your way back on your own to yet another hotel room, where you can guarantee there will not be enough of those little milk cartons'.

FEMALE FIRST

Loughborough Town Hall, 10 September: a venue and a date that don't mean a lot to most people but to Micky Flanagan they represented the biggest achievement of his comedic career. He had done his time on the comedy circuit and had worked hard, playing countless venues and had not taken any quick route to fame. In an interview, a few years later, he acknowledged that he was

pleased that he took the route he did and didn't fall for any get-famous-quick deals.

For Micky hadn't gone down the easy route to fame, it was sheer hard work and determination, and now he was about to embark on his first nationwide tour with Out Out, and the Town Hall in Loughborough on that unseasonably mild September evening was going to be his opening night.

Micky was ready with over 60 minutes of material to entertain and walked out on the stage in his now well-known stand-up 'uniform' of dark shirt and trousers. He was smart, he had a job to do and he wanted to do it well. He made no bones about the fact that the tour would be a culmination of his last two Edinburgh Festival shows but by combining the material and tweaking certain bits, he was sure he had an hour's worth of comedy gold up his sleeve.

'This is an unashamedly greatest hits show,' he told *Time Out* magazine. 'A bit like going to see Bob Dylan and him opening with "Maggie's Farm" and closing with "Like A Rolling Stone" and no wanking in between. However I am considering doing an electric version of my classic "Out Out" bit. Please don't call me Judas.'

The first show was a success and seven days later he was in Canterbury, entertaining audience members at the Gulbenkian theatre, before heading to Norwich to perform at the Playhouse.

As well as being live on stage, Micky was coming into

people's homes on the telly too and could be seen on episode three of *Comedy Central* at The Comedy Store on 18 September. It was a series that was comprised of 20 programmes of performances from one of the most famous venues in the country for live comedy and he appeared alongside Kai Humphries, Tom Wrigglesworth and Neil Delamere.

On 29 September he played The Glee club in Birmingham before heading to the chain's sister venue in Cardiff. At the beginning of October he was at Cornerstone Arts Centre in Didcot and the following day at the Colchester Arts Centre. On 3 October he performed at the Warwick Arts Centre in Coventry before heading to the New Milton Forest Arts Centre on the 8th and then the Palace Theatre in Southend on 9 October.

Visiting Southend-on-Sea brought back lots of memories for Micky as it was a place he used to go as a young man: he would get drunk, ride the waltzer and, if the tide was out, 'lay down on the mud'. When he was living in the East End, he and his mates would often go to Southend for a seaside break as it was easy to get to and offered a little bit of excitement and a change of scenery from the city. Travelling very far didn't ever excite Micky; as a youngster he would leave London and get to the beach and have a beer in his hand as quickly as possible.

'Michael Palin has nothing to worry about from me,' he told an interviewer in 2011. 'Southend was the seaside town of choice for us boys from the East End. What more

could you want? It's all there, you can get to Fenchurch Street in 20 minutes, you can be in Southend in an hour and 10, and be in the Foresters Pub by lunchtime. Then you can go to the Kursaal!' (Out Out)

The Kursaal was an amusement park with a range of funfair rides like the waltzer and bumper cars that a teenage Micky would enjoy. No coincidence then that when he returned to Southend again with his tour (this time performing at The Cliffs Pavilion) in 2011, he chose this destination to record his live show for the DVD.

'They asked me where I wanted to record the DVD, they said to me, "Do you want to go to the East End, the West End?" I said there was only one place to record the DVD – Essex!' Micky told those who'd come to see him for the Southend stage of the Out Out tour.

It was in direct contrast to some big-name comedians who often choose the largest and most exotic amphitheatre they can fill, such as Eddie Izzard playing Madison Square Garden, or Micky's teenage comedy icons, The Pythons, at the Hollywood Bowl.

The tour continued, as did various TV appearances, which had all been pre-recorded and were adding to Micky's exposure. He took part in Rhod Gilbert's BBC show, *Ask Rhod Gilbert*, which was a series that saw Rhod get to grips with a number of burning issues and hot topics posed by well-known personalities and members of the public. Micky joined Rhod and his regular panelists Greg Davis, Rhod's flatmate Lloyd

Langford and Carol Vorderman for the show, which was broadcast on Monday, 10 October. He also took part in Richard Bacon's *Beer & Pizza Club*, a chat show where guests eat pizza, drink beer and debate all of the issues that matter to the modern man. Micky joined Danny Wallace and Charlie Baker on the episode that was broadcast on Wednesday, 13 October. Two days later he could be seen performing at the Comedy Box theatre in Bristol, a venue he would sell out for two nights before moving on to Tonbridge Wells to perform at the Trinity Theatre on 22 October.

Each night he performed, he was doing the routine to a sell-out audience. There wasn't a spare ticket to be found and lots of venues were turning away disappointed fans as they were too late booking the tickets. Micky was as chuffed as anyone.

'I'd be lying to you if I said I wasn't surprised by it all, and I'm not in the business of lying,' he told the *Nottingham Post* in 2011. He went on:

I've reached the stage where I can go to most towns and sell out a decent-sized theatre. That's exciting for any stand-up. I did my time and learnt every trick in the book. I can say inappropriate things in front of a thousand people and they love it! I see the show as sanity in an insane world. The other night, I had a rant on stage about them charging 80p for a KitKat on trains, and I got a cheer. I thought, 'That's it. I've

connected'. Comedy needs focus and investment from the audience. It works best live.

On 29 October, at the Arts Centre in Swindon Micky performed to another sell-out crowd. His tour was in full swing and audience members loved how he could regale them with tales of times gone by interspersed with rude anecdotes on why the number of teenage pregnancies are so high – 'Teenagers don't know the art of fingering anymore.' He was also liberal with the words 'c**t' and 'f**k' but the audience loved it. They knew what they were getting with Micky: he was rude but truthful. He was cheeky, but laughed at himself as well as others. He told stories of being a middle-class drunk dipping bread in oil at middle-class dinner parties, then in the next breath, he was telling the audience how he had spent most of the eighties chasing women and doing drugs. Then he told them how he tried teaching – which didn't agree with him, and how he has tried to connect with the youth of today – the 'chicken children'. And of course, he built up to his Out Out gag. The audience were gagging for it, Micky knew it but he kept them waiting and after each line of the joke, he drew the crowd in before delivering another well-rehearsed line. At the end of the hour there was only one gag that Micky could end the night on, the one that the crowd had been anticipating all evening: the ketchup-in-the-restaurant gag.

At the beginning of November Micky had 12 dates

to play – on 4 and 5 November he was at Chesterfield Winding Wheel and 53 Degrees North in Preston. For the next four consecutive nights, 10–13 November, he was at Telford Oakengates Theatre, the Komedia club in Brighton, The Plough in Torrington and then to Maidenhead Nordon Farm Arts Centre. He had now been touring for two months and although the schedule wasn't overly gruelling, being away from his family was tough and Micky, however well used to being on the road, still found it hard going.

'Ultimately the performing is the best part of touring,' he told FemaleFirst website in 2011. 'But it also allows me to sort of see the UK, really. I know it sounds like a lame thing to say but it's just nice to arrive in cities and go for a walk around for a few hours. You're your own boss. Everything that you achieve is largely down to you getting up off your arse, writing good material and performing it. But the worst thing is that you're your own boss.'

He also had quite romantic visions of what touring would be like after watching one of his favourite comedians, Billy Connolly, do a documentary about his life, as he also explained in the *Female First* interview:

'I think in the morning they showed him [Billy] going out on his bike, the afternoon he did a bit of salmon fishing and in the evening he strolled off to the theatre to do his show. I watched and thought, that would be quite a nice life, that would do for me. Any version of that would be very, very nice. But I will say this, if you're the sort of

person who needs your friends and family around you on a daily basis, do not get into stand-up comedy.'

November continued with more travelling. On the 18th he entertained at Wrexham University before going on to Middlesborough Town Hall on the 19th and then the Grand Theatre in Lancaster on 20 November. On the 25th he performed at The Old Brook Theatre in Chatham and then two days later appeared in Wolverhampton. The demand for the show was increasing and Micky was asked if he could squeeze in another date in his November schedule and he duly obliged. The next two nights he performed once at The Slade Rooms and then at Wulfrun Hall in Wolverhampton.

It was the same situation when he performed at his next venue, The Lowry in Salford, on 29 November. The show was a sell-out and he agreed to play an extra date there at the beginning of January, the following year. This was only the tip of the iceberg, though. It was becoming clear to Micky, his management team and the tour promoters that people wanted to see him on tour and were fed up with not getting tickets as they were sold 'out out' so quickly. Something had to be done and the following year, in January 2011, it was announced that he would be adding an extra 21 dates to his spring tour, including an extra night at the Hammersmith Apollo. The popularity of his show also put to rest the concerns he had about performing his Cockney routine up and down the country, wondering if people who lived outside London would find

Top left: In his element, Micky is pictured here performing at the Greenwich Comedy Festival. © *REX Features*

Top right: Arriving at the Loaded LAFTA Awards in February 2012. © *PA Images*

Bottom left: On the Graham Norton sofa with Sir Alan Sugar, Cliff Richard and Kelly Rowland. © *PA Images*

Bottom right: Micky with Chelsea's John Terry in March 2014. © *PA Images*

Top left: Having a laugh with Barbara Windsor on *Chris Moyles' Quiz Night* in August 2011.

Top right: Pausing while the audience laughs on *Comedy Rocks with Jason Manford*.

Bottom: Making Miranda Hart hysterical on the set of *King Of*. © *REX Features*

Clockwise from top left: Micky with wife Cathy at the British Comedy Awards in December 2011; at a Channel 4 Comedy Gala at The O2 Arena; arriving at the Secret Policeman's Ball in New York with Jack Whitehall and Jimmy Carr; being presented with a commemorative plaque by General Manager of the O2 Rebecca Kane after selling out seven tour dates at the venue, performing to over 100,000 fans.

© *REX Features*

Top: Relaxing at one of his local pubs in East Dulwich, The Lordship Tavern.

© *REX Features*

Bottom left: Micky performing on stage during the Teenage Cancer Trust series of charity gigs at the Royal Albert Hall in March 2014. © *PA Images*

Bottom right: Making the ladies laugh on ITV's *Loose Women* in December 2013.

© *REX Features*

it as funny as those from the capital. But he didn't need to lose any sleep over it, the show was a success wherever he went, and he was touched by the warm reception he was receiving at all the venues he'd played so far.

'We [the management team and Micky] were concerned about the Lowry in Salford, whether anyone would turn up but we ended up selling five nights. They seemed to accept me as one of them even though I'm clearly from a council estate in London,' he told the *Portsmouth News* in 2011. 'When I play up north sometimes I do wonder if they think everyone from the south of England is a cockney. Their perception of London is often through TV and things like Del Boy so when I do my cockney walk, they find that very funny.'

The year was creeping by but there was no let-up in Micky's schedule – December was a busy month for him – not just for the planned live shows that he had to perform, but it was also the month that he was going to have to put on his best performance yet for a very special audience. It was time for the Cockney charmer to perform in the holy of holies when it came to theatre shows. Time for Micky to take to the stage and try and make the Royal Family laugh, at The Royal Variety Performance...

ROYALS AND RECOGNITION

'For a chap who has spent large parts of his life working hard for fairly low pay, I'm never going to harp on about the nightmare of touring; I'm a lucky man.'
BRISTOL POST

The Royal Variety Performance is an annual gala evening in which members of the Royal Family are entertained by a variety of acts – entertainers, comedians, musicians, acrobats, actors, theatre companies and solo performers. It is the crème de la crème of shows for anyone to perform in and brings together a range of eclectic talent.

Micky couldn't believe it when his agent rang with the news that an invitation had come through for him to perform at the Gala, although he joked with an interviewer from the *Northern Echo* that it was only a matter of time.

'I knew this day would come,' he joked. 'It was a

question of them scouring the planet for people they feel would be suitable. Then it's all hush-hush and seems to be done in café bars like spies and then you get sent a letter... and I didn't want to say no.'

The BBC had been in contact with Micky before the official invite came through, having been impressed with his guest appearances on the Richard Bacon and Rhod Gilbert shows. They wanted Micky, who was a new funny face on the circuit and was playing a sell-out tour on the billing for the 2010 show, and he was happy to oblige. And he couldn't wait to tell his mum either, as this was a show that the whole family used to watch together when he was a child. 'I remember watching it when I was a youngster in my pyjamas and it was a big deal back then,' he told the *Bristol Post* in 2011.

Micky went to a meeting with the BBC, who told him they were trying to re-vamp the show that year and encourage a new generation of people to watch it. They were inviting the likes of Kylie and N-Dubz to take part and wanted Micky, the man of the moment, to take part too.

But when you are dealing with such a high profile, family-friendly show, the pressure not to cause an upset or be too rude was clear to all performers, especially the comedians. There was a certain protocol that had to be followed and Micky knew that the bulk of the material from his Out Out tour wouldn't work as it was just too rude to perform. But while it made him re-think his material, he wasn't overly impressed at being told what

to do, adamant that he was not a rude comic, merely one who treats his audience as grown-ups. He was told by the producers that he had to run all his planned material past them and they made sure he was aware of royal protocol. So Micky had an opening gag planned – of asking Prince Charles if he wanted the palace windows cleaned as he obviously had the experience of being a window cleaner for many years. The punchline being that Micky would tell HRH that if he saw any crown jewels lying around, he couldn't guarantee that he wouldn't put them in his cleaning bucket! But in the end he didn't use it. Micky found that weeks before the show a lot of the material he submitted to the show's producers was edited and his ideas were either agreed upon or he was asked to come up with something else – they didn't want any upsets.

One of the other gags Micky had planned to deploy was one he had previously used on his Radio 4 show about the fact that what we in the UK call our bottoms, many Americans call their 'ass'; and that in Cockney speak, if he was referring to where he lived, he would call his home his ''ouse'. The way EastEnder Micky would pronounce ''ouse' was a lot like how an American would pronounce 'ass' so his gag consisted of a tale of his date with an American girl, during which he asked if there was any chance of coming in her ''ouse'. Of course the bosses decided that it was a little too rude – even though Micky argued such a play on words was just the kind of thing happily performed in the Carry On films only 20

years ago – with the result that he could have felt it a little frustrating to be true to himself as a comic and please the audience at the same time.

In 2011 he told the *Bristol Post*, 'I'm not a rude comic. I'm a realist who treats his audience like they are grown-ups. When I do my live shows I throw the book out of the window. But the minute you appear on TV or radio everything has to be scrutinised. Russell Brand and Jonathan Ross upset the applecart because we were getting into the position of a grown-up attitude where as long as you tell people before the show that it might offend it was OK. Why shouldn't people be allowed to watch provocative TV in the privacy of their own homes where they're trapped by children and can't get out?'

The 2010 Royal Variety Performance was held at The London Palladium on Thursday, 9 December, to be shown the following day on ITV1. Prince Charles and his wife Camilla, Duchess of Cornwall, were performing the royal duties that evening. But things didn't get off to a good start for the royal couple when they were caught up in a protest by angry students, who were holding a violent demonstration after the government passed a controversial new bill that saw university tuition fees treble to £9,000. Angry activists smashed a window of the royal car as they travelled to the venue, unexpectedly getting caught up in the protest. Neither Charles nor Camilla had been hurt in the fracas but security was tightened as they arrived at the venue.

Inside the atmosphere was buzzing and award-winning comedian Michael McIntyre, who was hosting the 82nd annual event, promised that it was going to be a night of high-class entertainment as the line-up included an array of big name stars. And he wasn't wrong. Take That, who were performing as a five-piece band for the first time since 1994, were due to perform two songs. Cheryl Cole would take to the stage to perform 'The Flood', an exclusive performance of the song from her second number one album, while Russell Watson was set to deliver a powerful performance of 'Parla Più Piano', best known as the love theme from *The Godfather*. N-Dubz and the Chelsea Pensioners would be singing, while the cast of *The Wizard of Oz* and *Les Misérables* performed pieces from their stage shows. Champion ice skater Daniel Whiston, two-time winner of ITV hit show, *Dancing On Ice*, would be performing a spectacular skating and flying routine. Plus the winners of that year's *Britain's Got Talent*, gymnastic troupe Spellbound, were the special performers of the night, having won the prestigious talent show earlier in the year and as first prize, earned themselves the right to perform for the Royal Family. Micky wasn't the only comedian in the line-up wanting to elicit some royal guffaws, though. John Bishop, Sarah Millican and Jack Whitehall would also perform solo stand-up routines for Their Royal Highnesses.

As the royal couple entered the foyer of the Palladium, as was tradition, they met some of the bigger acts that

were due to perform and that evening, even though they were still a little shaken from earlier events, they were all smiles as they were introduced to Kylie, Take That and N-Dubz.

Micky was scheduled to appear in the later part of the show after the Chelsea Pensioners had roused the audience to sing along with them and Daniel Whiston had performed his spectacular ice skating. Michael McIntyre had introduced Daniel so it was up to the voice-over to welcome him on to the stage. He came on and immediately started his act by introducing himself as the resident cockney and he performed his standard 'Cockney walk' across the stage, followed by his 'busy Cockney walk'. He then performed his 'chicken children' gag before launching into the ever-popular 'ketchup-in-the-restaurant' skit. It was his final joke before he finished his four-minute set and the audience loved it. He bowed to Prince Charles and Camilla, who had both looked suitably amused during his chicken children gag and walked off stage as it was time for the cast of *Les Misérables* to perform their set. It had been a successful evening for Micky and one he would never forget. Nor would his fans, who tweeted their praise of his performance once he had left the stage. @gray-I-am wrote: '*Micky Flanagan is bloody hilarious! I'll have the bottle pls! #**funnyasf**k #RVP*' while @Timcox wrote: '*Royal Variety just got funny thanks to cockney mick! #chicken child*'.

Micky spoke about the experience when he appeared

as a panelist on irreverent political quiz show *Have I Got News For You* the following year, telling fellow contestants:

'It was a great experience, although there is something a bit peculiar about standing in the wings watching a chap ice-skating and then the cast of *Les Mis* go on after you. I've been doing comedy for 12 years and the most I've ever followed is a bloke with a guitar. So that was all a bit odd!'

Normally once the show had concluded and the filming had finished, the royals would come and meet all the stars, who would be presented to them and shake their hands. But Prince Charles' security team decided that due to the trouble that had occurred on the journey to the venue, for safety reasons it was better to whisk them away straight after the show and so Micky and his fellow performers didn't get the chance to meet Charles or Camilla.

But Micky was upbeat as ever when he spoke about the missed opportunity the following week: 'We was all lined up to meet them but for security reasons they went. That was it, gone. Not even a goodbye. The really important people got to meet them beforehand. I didn't.'

But if he was questioning his own standing, and we doubt he really was, the fact that tickets for his tour were selling quicker than hotcakes was some indication of his popularity. At the beginning of December he was due to play three shows but the promoters wanted to squeeze one more out of him as fans were desperate to

see him and so he managed to add an extra date. On 2 December he was in Cambridge, at the arts theatre Up The Junction, and then it was time to head back to London, just over a week later. London was his hometown, the place he had played most of his gigs when starting out and the home of most of his friends and family. But it was a different London that Micky was about to see; his level of fame now was such that he had a sell-out show to perform at the Lyric Theatre on Shaftsbury Avenue. It was a venue well known in the West End for putting on some of the most popular shows in the entertainment business, including *Blood Brothers*, *Steel Magnolias*, *Cat On A Hot Tin Roof*, *Hairspray: The School Musical* and *Thriller Live*. Now it was time for Micky to fill the auditorium with fans eager to see him perform. The Lyric Theatre held 967 seats over four levels and on 13 December, the audience started pouring in off the wintry streets to treat themselves to a bit of pre-Christmas cheer. And they weren't disappointed, for when it came to reviews of the show on the Ticketmaster website, the praise could not have been better.

'Proper funny! I actually had tears and couldn't catch my breath at points during this performance. A show not to be missed. Already recommended to friends.' Five stars. Posted by LongMan.

'Very funny... Great mixture of improvised and written material, very funny and a proper showman.

Would recommend him to anyone.' Five stars. Posted by humedini.

'Flanagan Makes It To The West End. Unlike some comedians, Micky had entirely new material and performed for two hours. I've seen him at small gigs, The Comedy Store and now to a packed house "up west". He has been superb on every occasion. We were at the Lyric where "Thriller Live" is currently showing. Micky tried a moonwalk while talking about his dad, the Smooth Criminal. Highly recommend.' Five stars. Posted by Rcooke.

'Get Your Tickets now!!! I have seen a number of comedians live recently and this show at the Lyric was absolutely amazing, from the moment Micky walked on stage to the final encore. If you don't do anything else buy some tickets to a show near you, I promise you will have the best night of your life!' Five stars. Posted by Rudga.

There was no doubting Micky's success now. The fans loved him and he himself was getting a buzz out of performing for audiences of such vast numbers. This was what he had worked so hard to achieve and he was enjoying every second of it.

'Am I successful? I think you measure your success by the people standing in front of you at a gig,' he admitted to the *Bristol Post* the following spring. 'When you start out playing to 20 people above a pub and then suddenly

you're walking out to the Lyric Theatre to 1,000 people, that's special and that's your success.'

And it wasn't just the fans wanting a piece of the forty-eight-year-old either. TV bosses were keen to book Micky after his successful Royal Variety Performance and on 16 December, he went along to the London Studios in Waterloo to film a special Christmas edition of the longest-running satirical panel shows on TV, *Have I Got News For You*. In 2011 the series received the Lifetime Achievement Award at the British Comedy Awards, the first time the honour had been bestowed on a programme rather than an individual.

Ian Hislop and Paul Merton have been on the panel since the show started in 1990 and each week are joined by a guest to have fun with the news topics of the week. Each episode takes over an hour to film. The audience filed into studio 2, the second largest of the studio centre, and took their seats, waiting for the panel to arrive. Alexander Armstrong was the guest host for the evening (he currently holds the record for the most appearances as guest presenter), while Ross Noble would be joining Ian Hislop's team for the show. Ross also holds the record for the most number of times a guest has been on the show, so it was just Micky who was the newbie for this special festive edition. Not that you would have realised. The set was decorated with tinsel and the background newspapers behind the panelists were decorated with Christmas graffiti. All panelists and the host were in

special Christmas jumpers for the recording, with Ian jokingly telling the audience while they were having their microphones wired up that 'they were allowed to choose their own clothes this evening'.

Micky had just had a haircut for the show and sat next to Paul Merton in a green jumper with a snowman on the front. All 'contestants' were decorated with woollen elves, reindeer, etc. Alexander made the introductions and described Micky as 'A comedian who went down a storm at the Royal Variety Performance and Prince Charles wet himself... on the way there. Please welcome Micky Flanagan!'

The first topic of discussion was the Royal Variety Performance and the violent demonstration that occurred beforehand and Micky made a joke straight away that Camilla was obviously 'well trained not to have bolted when she was poked with a stick.' It got the audience laughing and he visibly relaxed.

The show was a success and over 2 million viewers tuned in to watch episode 10 of series 40. Micky wasn't as vocal as fellow panelist Ross or team captains Ian and Paul, and tried to slip in a few one-liners but was drowned out a couple of times by Paul. But he did announce halfway through the show that he was getting a bit hot in his Christmas jumper. So Ross told him he could take off his trousers if he wanted to, to which Micky replied, 'I have already.'

He played with his newly trimmed hair when he did

speak, which might have indicated a certain nervousness, but he did look as if he was enjoying himself on the panel. And why wouldn't he? Here he was on a 'high-brow' comedy show based upon quick reactions to the topics in the news and for a kid who had left school with no qualifications to hold his own among these three seasoned practitioners was no mean feat.

After the recording of *HIGNFY*, Micky was able to take a couple of days off for Christmas and put his feet up for a well-earned rest before his tour started again in the New Year. There was still one more gig to 'perform' before 2010 was over, though, and it was going to be a big one. Micky's audiences were growing by each gig and on Tuesday, 28 December, fans tuned in to BBC1 at 10.35pm to watch him perform one of his biggest TV gigs yet. Micky was performing in the BAFTA-nominated *Live At The Apollo*. It was the penultimate episode of series 6 and he had recorded the show back in October, as was the norm for such shows since recordings took place two or three months before they were due to air.

The Hammersmith Apollo is one of the biggest entertainment venues in London and has played host to a number of legendary performers, including The Beatles, The Rolling Stones, Bob Marley, Elton John, Kylie Minogue, Peter Kay, Oasis, REM and Stereophonics, to name but a few. Russell Brand, Jimmy Carr, Sean Lock and Jason Manford are all big-name comics who have performed solo gigs in front of the over 3,000-seater

audience and now it was time for Micky to strut his cockney stuff on stage. Stephen K Amos was the host for the evening and his guest comedians performing their sets were Jon Richardson and Micky.

Micky walked out centre stage in dark blue shirt and black trousers and immediately played his cockney walk gag before talking about his time as an 'international player in the 1980s'. He then talked about dating in the eighties and how he would woo a woman with a Steak Diane and prawn cocktail. It wasn't his usual line-up of gags but the material wasn't new, it was stuff he had adapted from his 'What Chance Change?' show and the audience was lapping it up.

Performing on the BBC didn't muffle his rude streak, either: he was playing to a grown-up crowd after the watershed and as such he decided to give his 'vagina stories' an airing. He went through the angry vagina, the Marxist one that growled before going through his experiences of pulling women in his bedsit (not council) and then it was time to bring out the kimono. He used the stage to its full advantage and went out to the side wings to illustrate him then approaching in full seductive mode in his dragon kimono. Presenter Esther Rantzen was in the audience and filmed laughing, especially when Micky told the story of looking after his son and becoming hooked on watching *Thomas the Tank Engine*. It was 11 minutes of stand-up that his fans would not have been overly familiar with, which made it all the more popular. Clips of the

show went up on YouTube and it received over half a million hits in record time. It might not have been Micky's usual gags but the viewers liked it all the same.

'Not very often in tears with laughter but Micky made my stomach hurt, I was laughing so much,' wrote Andy Paddock. 'It tops "the chicken children,"' while kaarateprincess1 merely commented: 'Angry vagina! What you lookin at?! ROFL.'

Micky was able to have a bit of a break after Christmas as the next live performance for his tour wasn't until 28 January at the Warwick Arts Centre. But that wasn't to say that he had disappeared from public consciousness altogether. Oh, no! And if people thought he was merely a funny Cockney guy, they were about to discover that he was a funny Cockney guy with a master mind too...

Chapter 11

MASTER(MIND)
OF COMEDY

'Seeing yourself on TV, or having some bloke come up to you
in the pub saying, "I saw you on the telly the other night"
doesn't feel like success. That feels a bit odd. You can't build a
career out of people saying hello to you in the street.'
BRISTOL POST, 2011

*C*elebrity *Mastermind* is the spin-off of the long-
running quiz show *Mastermind*, with the format
being nearly identical – the theme music and the same
black chair in which the contestants sit is the same and
John Humphrys acts as quizmaster for both. The only
difference between the two shows is that the questions are
easier for the celebrities. Contestants have two minutes to
answer questions about their specialist subject and then
two minutes to respond to general knowledge questions.
Previous contestants on the show, which has been running

since 2003, include Jeremy Beadle, Lembit Opik, Gok Wan, Mick Hucknall, Paul O'Grady, Stephen Fry, John Bishop and Beverley Knight.

The eighth series of the show, which started raising money for Children In Need on 19 November, returned for 10 nights at the end of December and beginning of January. Viewers tuning in to the final show on Friday, 7 January 2011 had the pleasure of watching *Strictly Come Dancing* star Kristina Rihanoff, BBC property show presenter Martin Roberts, former *Bill* actress Seeta Indrani and the man himself, Micky Flanagan, take part. Yep, Micky's management team had received the invite to ask if the comedian would like to participate in the show. The answer didn't take long to decide, 'Bosh yes!' But Micky was careful in choosing his specialist subject as he didn't want to look like a fool on national TV – or in front of his mates at the pub!

'*Mastermind* is the most intense interrogation you can get, with 7m viewers and the possibility of looking a complete fool. I didn't want to get one wrong and spend the rest of my life walking into a pub and having that one repeated to me.'

So what was his specialist subject? It was the life and music of Bruce Springsteen. Micky has been a life-long fan of the legendary American musician and it was a relatively easy topic for him to answer questions on because he was obsessed with the songs from 'The Boss'. A lot of Springsteen's songs struck a chord with Micky as two of

his most successful albums, *Born to Run* and *Born in the U.S.A.*, find grandeur in the struggles of daily 'blue collar' American life. Micky spoke of how he'd love to be in a band with Bruce in an interview with Jongleurs website, years later.

'If I was the lead singer in a band, I'd call mine, "Them And Us". I've always liked bands with ridiculous names. I remember there was a Northern Irish band in the sixties called Them. Although I can't really sing, to be honest. I might have a go in the shower or round the house, but I'm not sure I could charge for it. That's the difference. And I would definitely have Bruce Springsteen in the band. Bruce on guitar would be a safe bet. I'd feel pretty comfortable knowing he was behind me if it all went tits up.'

As the lights dimmed in the *Mastermind* studio, Micky watched as *Homes Under The Hammer* presenter Martin Roberts answered questions on the cartoons of Hanna-Barbera but didn't get off to a good start, scoring a mere six with three passes. Next up was Kristina Rihanoff, who was answering questions about the life and career of Patrick Swayze and doubled Martin's score by getting an impressive 13 points with 4 passes. Micky was the last celebrity to take the hot seat that night and watched as Seeta Indrani answered questions on her specialist subject, the operas of Giacomo Puccini. It was an impressive performance and she scored 18 points, with no passes. Then it was Micky's turn and he looked relatively at ease in the spotlight to answer questions on Bruce. He didn't

embarrass himself either and scored an impressive 13 points but with no passes, ensuring he would have another break before returning for the general knowledge round.

In the GK round, Martin scored a lot better and finished the show on a respectable 18 points. Kristina had to answer only six questions correctly to beat him, which she just did, and finished on 20 points. The competition was now between Micky and Seeta, and Micky showed that he was no ignoramus by scoring 12 points, again with no passes. He had a total of 25 and Seeta didn't manage to match his general knowledge round score but she did get enough to finish winner of the night with 28 points.

Finishing second was a big achievement for Micky and more importantly, as it was *Celebrity Mastermind*, all the celebrities were playing to raise money for the charity of their choice. He announced at the beginning of his specialist round that he would be donating his appearance fee to the Kids Company charity. The organisation was founded in 1996 to provide practical, emotional and educational support to vulnerable inner-city children and young people. Looking out for over 36,000 children across London and Bristol, the charity operates through a network of drop-in centres, alternative education centres and over 40 school and he was proud to be raising money and awareness for such a worthy cause.

On 13 January there was welcome news from Micky's management team for all his fans who had been disappointed about not being able to see his show – there

were going to be an extra 21 dates added to his Out Out tour to keep up with popular demand. The fans were happy, the tour promoters were happy, and Micky too was happy – and ready to work as hard as he could to meet the demand. He was eager to strike while the iron was hot, and people wanted to come and see him perform.

'It's a lot of dates but it's not really hard work,' he revealed in an interview with the *Bristol Post* in 2011. 'The worst thing you can do as a stand-up is book a tour that doesn't sell. That's the nightmare scenario. So to be able to sell out a load of dates and add more is great. The promoters are so pleased with how well the tour's selling that they've been scouring the UK for more venues.'

At the beginning of the tour in September 2010, Micky was due to end his run of Out Out by 23 March 2011. As it stood, the extra dates added meant that he would be touring the country until the end of April. Little did he know at that point that the final finish date would be a lot later, but for now it was time to throw himself back into work and that is exactly what he did, kicking off 2011 by slotting in an extra tour date at the Anvil in Basingstoke on 27 January before heading to the planned Warwick Arts Centre on the 28th and then the Lowry in Salford again on the 29th.

From the 3–7 February it was a nightly performance in different venues, meaning that Micky would travel straight after a gig to get to the next venue before grabbing a few hours' kip, getting his bearings and then performing

again. Driving himself in his trusty Toyota Verso, he made his way from the St Albans Arena (where he performed to over 800 fans) to the Cambridge Corn Exchange and then on to the Grand Opera House in York.

At every venue the audience reviews were pretty much in agreement – Micky was hilarious. Ticketmaster carried such comments as: 'What an underrated comedian. Really, really funny. Nuff said,' posted by janettegirlie; 'The funniest thing I've seen in a long time. I laughed so much my jaw ached. Highly recommend,' posted by Rosey85; while JBJOHN posted that 'once again Micky was superb. Followed Micky for nearly 10 years now and saw him last time he was in York, in a basement. He is absolute quali...tie.'

The conclusions were the same everywhere Micky went, people were laughing until they were crying, the material had something to suit everyone and you got good value for money – with the average ticket price around £16, he would be on stage for a good hour and a half and people were impressed.

After leaving York he headed to Birmingham Town Hall and then on to Salisbury City Hall before getting a couple of days' rest in between.

'I've always done really well in the Midlands,' he told the *Resident* newspaper in an interview in 2013. 'One of my favourite places to play is Birmingham, where the audiences are really appreciative. Warwick is fantastic and in Nottingham they just accept you. They aren't

bothered about you being a Londoner as long as you are funny. Although when I play Newcastle I do wonder if they think anyone from the south of England is a cockney. The idea of people in Derbyshire or Lancaster being different to Londoners is all in your head. The world now is very small.'

His next gig, on 10 February, was in Southend again but this time he would be performing at The Cliffs Pavilion (a venue he would also be returning to two more times later in his extended tour). The Cliffs Pavilion would be the venue where he would record the DVD for the tour and he made sure the audience knew how lucky they were when he walked out on stage and opened the show with the news:

'The tour people, they asked me, they said, "Mick, where do you wanna go for the DVD? Do you want to go East? Do you want to go West?"' He paused for effect. 'And I said, I wanna go to Essex! The only way is Essex!' and the crowd roared with approval. There were several other references to *The Only Way Is Essex* during the show, Micky was taking the er, micky, out of the popular ITV2 fly-on-the-wall show, *TOWIE*, which saw young, glamorous, fake-tanned men and women strut their stuff on telly, apparently oblivious to the cameras capturing their every move.

There were several hecklers that Micky sparred with, as well as telling the audience that because he'd 'f**ked up' one gag, he was going to do it again and they had better

laugh in the right place as the performance was going to DVD. Needless to say, after being ribbed that they were obviously good at acting, as Micky had seen on *TOWIE*, the audience didn't let him get away with it that easily and he told them off for mucking up his recording. But his easy, familiar manner was clear and for those who didn't get to see him live, the DVD would offer the chance of seeing just how 'normal' he was while making the most mundane things seem funny; he really could connect with his audience.

'My material is pretty upbeat,' he told the *Bristol Post* interviewer while on his Out Out tour. 'Comedy is largely about telling some sort of truth. Because of who I am and where I come from, it wouldn't work if I came on and said something cynical or shocking.'

It probably wasn't too much of a surprise that at the beginning of January 2011, Micky's name was the most searched for comedian's name on ticketing websites according to *Hitwise*. They reported that in the week ending 22 January, the British public made him more popular than Michael McIntyre, Lee Evans and Peter Kay by searching for his comedy gig tickets the most. The top ten list was as follows: 1. Micky Flanagan, 2. Sarah Millican, 3. Greg Davis, 4. Lee Evans, 5. Peter Kay, 6. Russell Howard, 7.Alan Carr, 8. Michael McIntyre, 9. Miles Jupp and 10. John Cleese.

Following the successful recording of the DVD in Southend, it was time for Micky to jump back in his

Verso and head for Bristol, where he would be taking his show to the Colston Hall, followed by Peterborough the day after to play the Cresset. He then had a mere five days' break to go back home and spend some time with Cathy and his son Max, who was now five years old, before heading for the West Sussex coast to play in the seaside town of Worthing on 18 February. Heading along the coastline he travelled to Bournemouth the following day and then on to Woking, to the New Victoria Theatre. Each venue was a sell-out and he didn't disappoint his fans. Following his Surrey gig, he then headed to Bromley, to the Theatre Royal, before taking his place on stage at the 1,700-capacity Southampton Guildhall. It was then a non-stop cycle of gig/travel/gig/travel as he journeyed from Reading (25 February) to Hastings (26th) to the Milton Keynes Theatre (27th) and then the Buxton Opera House on the 28th. On Sunday the 27th he also found time to appear on *Something For The Weekend* on BBC1 and although looking a little sleepy from the night before – he admitted to going out out for a few drinks after his gig – the resident chef, Simon Rimmer, made him a Monmouth pudding, which he said afterwards, 'sorted him out'.

March was as relentless, from the 3rd he appeared at four gigs on the trot, travelling from Crawley to Leeds to Nottingham and then Aylesbury's Waterside Theatre for a two-night stint. The *Daily Telegraph* decided to visit the Buckinghamshire theatre on 6 March to review the tour and gave it a five out of five in their culture review

section. It was Micky's 'common touch that crosses all social barriers' that made his show such a success, they suggested:

> At last year's Royal Variety Performance, Micky Flanagan made the Prince of Wales laugh with a routine about why today's teenagers keep asking "what's happenin'?" It's always nice to see Prince Charles momentarily helpless with mirth, reminding us that he's one of us, able to get the joke and all that but the moment absolutely encapsulates why a normal-looking cockney geezer with frizzy hair and a goonish grin is doing so phenomenally well, constantly adding dates to keep up with demand. Cheap enough to do crowd-pleasing smut and scatological gags, he's also bold enough to push ideas, arguments and theories his audience's way. A jack of all trades then, and a breath of fresh air.

The *Telegraph* wasn't the first publication to note that some of Micky's material had a slight political message to it, even though it was done within the boundaries of comedy and he certainly wasn't preaching to the audience. Micky knows the importance of not attempting to score party-political points, despite being 'firmly on the left'.

'I think comedians are always worried whether their comedy will change things or make a difference,' he admitted to the *Telegraph* in 2013. 'My contract with the

people who come to see me is that I make them laugh first and foremost. If that doesn't happen all the messages in the world are going to be meaningless. If I make people laugh a lot and I slip in a few of those bits, fine. But not at the expense of making them laugh.'

Similarly, in an interview with the *Independent* in 2011, he spoke about why he keeps his jokes about politics to a minimum now. 'I avoid too much of the red flag flying because many fans don't want to hear it or don't agree with it. I did a bit about discussing the seventies with the audience in Edinburgh and I remarked, "and then Thatcher came along and it all went tits up!" Only about 50 of the 2,000-strong audience laughed. That's your ratios now. They don't mind you doing a Blakey impression [part of his gag about making his son watch *On The Buses*] but you can't be having a go at Thatcher!'

Micky quotes Soren Kierkegaard, a nineteenth-century Danish philosopher, in his act when he talks about how the best adults take the longest to grow up. It's a saying that he uses to great effect that is mostly lost on the audience when he's doing a gag about answering the phone and trying not to put on a Chinese accent 'just for a laugh'. But this idea does hold quite a resonance with him: 'Life can only be understood backwards; but it must be lived forwards.'

On 9 March there was a break from the tour for some promotional duties and he was invited to Steve Wright's Radio 2 show that afternoon to be interviewed. He joined

Steve, Tim Smith and Janey Lee Grace and spoke of his love of Thomas the Tank Engine; he also met Peter Kay and interior designer Linda Barker, who were on the show. On 10 March he went to Bristol Colston Hall and then St Albans the following night, before making his solo debut at London's Hammersmith Apollo. Appearing at the venue the previous year for the BBC's *Live At The Apollo* helped Micky prepare for his own tour – he would be revisiting it for two more sell-out nights later that month. But walking out in front of a venue that seats over 3,500 people was still pretty daunting for the forty-six-year-old. There was one person in the audience who would be feeling particularly proud of his performance, his dad. After seeing him perform years ago when he came second in the *Hackney Empire Act of the Year*, he was incredibly proud of his son. He didn't even mind that Micky would use him as the butt of his jokes, frequently referring to his dad's behaviour in the seventies as a drunk and a chancer. That was Micky's act and his dad didn't mind, but it was a marginally different matter when it came to his wife.

'My wife doesn't like me telling you she's a crap shag but makes a good sandwich,' he told the audience at his Southend gig. 'But I always tell her what I'm going to be talking about. I run all this past her.' The wives of professional comedians quite often get a raw deal when it comes to being the butt of jokes but Cathy didn't mind. She was used to her husband and his child-like humour and Micky admitted, when doing promotional interviews

for his tour, two years later, that he changed his tack slightly by not mentioning her directly in his gags.

'I won't say "my wife..." I say, "Isn't it funny that as you get older a dirty weekend turns into a very restful break?"'

He told presenter Graham Norton, when he appeared on his show in 2013, that he was very lucky that Cathy had such a great sense of humour, but he would never push things or 'cross the line between being funny or revealing too much'.

'We do have to discuss it [the jokes] a lot, but I just go out and make the jokes anyway when she's not at the show. No, seriously, I'm very lucky. In life you have to find someone in your life with a great sense of humour and who is very cool, which she is, but we do have to have lines that we don't cross. I would never put anything sexual in the show about her... we've only done it twice anyway!'

And there were certain topics that he has often said he wouldn't joke about in his routines, and it would quite often depend on who was in the audience. It's no secret that he is quite a tell-it-like-it-is comic but he doesn't feel that comedy should be at the expense of the audience. Especially when they have paid to come and watch him perform! Although risk is a big part of his stand-up routine, he is very much a comic who is aware of his audience. He has a general rule that he sticks to, about not telling a joke if the victim of his joke is someone in

the audience, for example. He told *Time Out* magazine: 'Say you have a great fat people routine but choose to drop it because there is an obese lady in the front row, then drop the material. Maybe come up with some good anorexia stuff. My instincts tell me not to go to certain places because a) I don't need to and b) I'm not the sort of comic who feels the right to establish that line with the audience. I don't do it in life, so why do it on stage.'

A couple of years later he also talked in an interview with *GQ Magazine* about the topics that are still off-limits when performing his shows, changing his tack slightly by commenting that most things can be joked about, if done professionally.

> I don't think any joke is off-limits if it's put in the right context and it's done with intelligence. It's just when it's thrown in and horrible and hurtful: that's when everyone gets upset. There's a lot of people getting upset on other people's behalf. You've got journalists getting offended on behalf of an entire race and they take on the good fight for them. It's a bit like whenever I see anyone from the East End portrayed as sort of shifty and crafty. Yes, there are some like that. I don't start going, 'There are no dishonest people in the East End! This is outrageous!'

The Apollo was ready for Micky, and Micky was ready for the Apollo. He was sold out for two nights and

coming to the end of one of his busiest months of the tour (there were still many more hectic months to come) and he was ready to take the London audience back to the East End of the seventies and eighties. The response was as expected. 'Gut-wrenchingly hilarious,' shouted the *Mirror*. 'Excellent, funny and poignant,' confirmed the *Observer*. 'Side-splitting,' agreed *The Sunday Times*. While the *Independent*, who reviewed the show on the second night, wrote: 'There's a good reason for the extra spring in the step of Micky Flanagan's signature cockney walk this evening. After nearly 15 years in comedy, and jobs before that which have included fish-packer and dish-washer, the Bethnal Green-bred 46-year-old was strutting out on to the stage of a venue that seats over 3,500 people and is synonymous with career ascendancy.'

And audience members, who paid less than £20 for a ticket, certainly got their money's worth. Micky found that performing to a larger audience meant a physical change of approach – he had to move around the stage a lot more to make sure he was speaking to all areas of the venue. But to say that was a problem was silly, there was no way that he was going to make moving around a drawback to his newfound success. He was loving every minute – and so too was the audience. In fact, one of the only real differences he found was that in a larger venue, the audience laughter reverberates around the room and the noise takes a long time to die down! Micky used this time to wander around the stage a lot more, something

you notice in his bigger arena gigs. He is playing to the audience, walking around and enjoying the laughter and waiting for the laughter to stop – and he wasn't going to cut short the laughter by talking over it or starting his next gag, he was ready to milk it for all it was worth! Ultimately, the only difference in the shows was that they would last a lot longer – not that anyone would complain about that, of course.

In an interview with *GQ Magazine* in 2013, he remarked, 'The first time you play a bigger venue it hits you. There's a sense of an outer body experience. But when we turned up at the Apollo for our little run there, I do remember thinking, this is exciting. Because not only were the audience really up for it, but I was on fire. It was one of those electric gigs. I remember thinking, this is probably as good as it gets. One of the hard things in the bigger venues is if you hit a joke really well and everyone's laughing, it is quite a long time until they stop.'

There was no time for Micky to bask in his success in one of London's top arenas, though. He still had people up and down the country buying tickets for his tour at a phenomenal rate and that meant after the second night at the Apollo he came straight off stage and packed up his bits to travel to Sheffield on 28 March, before heading to Nottingham on the 29th and Birmingham Symphony Hall on 31 March.

Always in contact with the fans via his Facebook page, he asked their opinion about his intro music and asked

for 'any suggestions for great choons to stick on before I tread the boards?' The comments ranged from 'anything by Chas and Dave' to 'Hey Micky' by Toni Basil, 'Maybe It's Because I'm a Londoner' and 'Till Death Us Do Part', the theme tune of Alf Garnett.

March was originally planned to be the end of the 59-date tour around the UK that had started in September 2010, but the British public had other ideas. They wanted more and that meant Micky was back in his Toyota Verso, heading off to Southend again at the beginning of April. And little did he know at this point that he would end up performing in nearly three times the original number of gigs by the close of 2011. People were coming 'out out' to watch him and he was ready!

Chapter 12

PERFORMANCES, PUBLICITY AND 'PLAGIARISM'

'*I would say to anybody who wants to be a comedian to get a very thick skin early on and also just do it. Try not to think about it too much. If you get on stage you will figure out what people find funny about you but that can only happen on stage. You won't have that eureka moment working in a call centre or sitting on the couch watching* Deal or No Deal.'

ENTERTAINMENT.IE

April and May 2011 proved to be a blur of performances across the country as Micky's Out Out tour grew ever more popular. He never showed signs of fatigue or boredom, though: this was what he had spent years working on, getting his act right and performing it in a certain way so as to get maximum effect from each gag. Over his years of playing the smaller pubs and comedy clubs he had learnt what various audiences find funny and

what they don't. There was no doubting that he made the job of being a stand-up look easy enough, but what Micky was doing on stage each time he performed his set for over an hour to hundreds of people a night was perform in a very co-ordinated, very rehearsed manner. He knew what worked and what didn't, and he was using that framework to make his tour a sell-out.

'Everyone has a few bits of a routine that people for some reason don't get,' Micky revealed to *GQ* in 2013. 'And you just think, "Oh, you idiots!" But then you can't start saying, "Stop! You're laughing at the wrong bit!" There are a number of bits that I've tried over the years that have fallen on deaf ears. One of the things that I've seen comics do is talk about football and it's the kiss of death, because half of the people go "not interested," and a quarter of them go, "Oh, it's a bit funny," but a lot of them just go, "I don't want to hear about football."'

In fact, Micky himself fell into this category. He wasn't a big football fan – although he loved playing it as a child – and despite being from the East End, where the Hammers were the footie team of choice, he only made it to the occasional game to watch Chelsea if his mates dragged him along.

'I've tried to be a football fan. I thought, "This is what men do." But I'm not. When it's exciting it's fine, but put it this way; if a game clashes with *Homeland* there's no competition,' he told Jongleurs website. 'My mate got me a ticket to see Chelsea a couple of weeks ago. It was my first

time in 20 years and I just sat there and felt nothing. The Bayern game was fun though, and it was a no-brainer when it went to penalties, as John Terry wasn't able to take part.'

Of course there were some nights when audience participation was a large part of the show and other performances when he would only get heckled once in the evening. Word spread on the internet from people who had seen his show that if you didn't want to get picked on, avoid sitting in the front two rows of the venue as that is where Micky likes to focus his audience interaction. Heckling wasn't quite so common, he was the one in charge of the show and could pick and choose who he wanted to ignore if he was heckled – not that he wasn't used to a rowdy crowd. His years of playing the pubs and clubs with an audience of 20 comedy fans soon put him in his place early on. But things were different now.

'Do people still heckle me?' Micky mused to entertainment.ie in 2013. 'Not at this level. If anything you might get someone very drunk and calling out something unnecessary and random. I had somebody shout the other night, "I'm getting married." I said to her, "Well, I'm sorry to hear that but we can't all live happy lives." It is a bit of excitement.'

Cambridge, Stoke and Southport were next on Micky's tour dates on 2, 5 and 6 April and on the 7th he found himself in Liverpool. If he had been concerned whether his 'crafty cockney' jokes would stand the test of geography he shouldn't have worried, the scousers loved him.

'Micky Flanagan has gratified crowds night after night and without a hint of exhaustion, he took to the Liverpool Empire stage, thanking the crowd for venturing "out out" mid-week, promising to be done by 10pm so "we can all get our eight hours" and instantly won us over with his impression of a cockney swagger,' wrote www.clickliverpool.com. 'Sharp, well crafted and, most importantly, laugh-a-minute material, not a single person in the crowd would have minded losing a few minutes before the alarm clock rang out this morning had he stayed on stage beyond 10pm but true to his word, he left the stage at 9.57pm to rousing applause after serving up an encore of his famous "Out Out" routine.'

Straight after Liverpool it was time for Micky to get back on the road to Salford again, where he would once more be appearing at the Lyric Theatre before heading to Cardiff on the 9th and then a long drive back south to the seaside town of Brighton to play at the Brighton Dome on the 10th. Then he had a couple of days off before travelling to Margate on the 13th and on 14 April he was in Blackpool, often described by the tourist industry as 'the Las Vegas of the North', thanks to its bright lights (the Blackpool Illuminations), all-night casino action (the Pleasure Beach is one of the most visited tourist attractions in the UK) and dazzling stage shows (the Winter Gardens is home to 12 different venues including a theatre, ballroom and conference facilities and hosts live shows and cabaret nights).

PERFORMANCES, PUBLICITY AND 'PLAGIARISM'

Micky would be performing at the Winter Gardens, in The Opera House, one of the country's largest theatres that has a seating capacity of almost 3,000 and has played host to some of the greats from the world of showbiz; from legends like Frank Sinatra, Judy Garland and Bob Hope to more modern superstars like JLS and One Direction. Many of the most popular touring shows have graced the stage too, like *Grease*, *Cats* and *Calendar Girls*.

As well as treating audience members to an hour of comedy delight, Micky could now reveal details of his DVD release, telling his fans that his debut DVD, the DVD of the Out Out tour, would be available to buy in the autumn and if they were really keen, they could pre-order it on Amazon!

The rest of April saw him visit Newcastle, Scarborough, Norwich, Basingstoke, Reading and Croydon. May held much the same schedule as before: from 3–6 May he performed in Peterborough, Northampton, St Alban Arena and then back to Southend again, The Cliff Pavilions, where he had been just a month earlier. He then had a well-deserved five-day break and spent some time with his son, who would be heading to school later that year, and Cathy, who was getting used to sharing her husband with thousands of comedy fans who also wanted to spend a night with him – in the entertainment sense only, of course!

On 11 May he was back at work and performed at Wolverhampton Civic Centre and the following day

headed to Chatham for an evening entertaining the audience at the Central Theatre. Pre-orders of his DVD were growing by the week and even though the release was still six months away, Micky's fans didn't want to miss out. It was a five-day break for the comic and then five days of consecutive gigs – Cambridge Corn Exchange (17th), Croydon Fairfield Halls (18th), Milton Keynes Theatre (19th), Bournemouth BIC (20th) and Cheltenham Racecourse on 21 May. Micky got in the spirit of the racing venue by telling his Facebook fans that he was 'thinking I might put a monkey on me being placed in the 5:15 hurdles. What's the strangest bet you've ever won?'

His Facebook page was a way of letting the fans know what he was up to, what TV shows he'd be appearing on, and getting their opinions on all sorts of matters. With over a quarter of a million 'likes' for his page, he regularly updated his fans with posts on his antics and tour information.

On 27 May he hit the Warwick Arts Centre and then travelled to Leicester to appear at the De Montfont Hall on 1 June. That month he would also be making more TV appearances, his second on *Mock The Week* on 16 June (alongside Chris Addison, Ed Byrne and Diane Morgan) and then again at the end of the month, on 30 June (alongside Alun Cochrane, Milton Jones and Zoe Lyons). His fans loved the telling of his vest story when he was given the topic of fashion by the spinning wheel of news in the earlier episode (coincidentally he also had

'fashion' as his stand-up topic when he appeared on the show the following year) and they were pleased to see him appear just a week later in the episode that aired on 7 July (alongside Ed Byrne, Milton Jones and Jack Whitehall). His third appearance did cause some controversy the following month when he went back on the show for the fifth episode of series 10. On the show, which was broadcast on Thursday, 7 July, Micky told the audience of his frustration at going to a U2 concert and seeing Bono invite the audience to sing along. 'Bono keeps saying, "Come on, join in, you know this one,"' he told Dara O Briain and the panel. 'I paid £25 to get in here and you're getting about a quarter of a million quid – you sing it.'

The gag, quite rightly, got a fair few chuckles from the studio audience but Micky didn't realise at the time that it had caused quite a stir on the social media sites – *Australia's Got Talent* hopeful Jordan Paris was vilified for telling the joke when he performed on the show, repeating word for word the gag that Lee Mack had first made famous. It caused a massive controversy Down Under: Jordan had made it to the semi-finals with his gags and footage showed him using several of Lee's jokes, as well as those of American comedian Geoff Keith. The fact that Micky had also used the same joke didn't go unnoticed by some of his fans.

'Micky is a headline act so should know better. He deserves to be dragged over the coals,' wrote one disgruntled fan on Chortle's forum.

But Micky's agent, Christian Knowles, was keen to point out that he was unaware of the gag being in dispute.

'Micky's not a plagiarist,' he told Chortle. 'It's a gag that he stopped doing about 10 years ago but went back to it because it worked with the topics on that episode of *Mock The Week*. Comedians do independently come up with similar ideas/jokes but because of the coverage regarding the contestant on *Australia's Got Talent* it made it appear that Micky has nicked the gag, this simply isn't true.'

It was a short-lived furore (if it was even that) and Micky announced that there would be a further 20 dates added to his UK tour and tickets would go on sale on 1 July. He also announced, via his publicist, that he would be taking up residence at the Garrick Theatre in London's West End that autumn and although only planned for a week-long stint, due to its overwhelming popularity the show was extended by a further week. Previously it had been announced that Micky would be playing nightly from 26 September to 8 October but now another five nights were added, which meant that he would be showcasing his Out Out tour until 15 October. The 18-night run tickets went on sale and ranged from £22.50 to £40 and sold out within weeks of being released.

At the end of May, filming took place in the O2 Arena for Channel 4's *Comedy Gala*. It was the second one that had been done by the broadcaster and gathered the biggest names in British comedy to perform on stage in succession

and would raise money for London's Great Ormond Street Hospital. Billed as 'the biggest live stand-up show in UK history', the show featured 17 top-class comedians who would be performing their own short sketches, as well as a number of other performers and entertainers with pre-recorded links and sets. The line-up for the 2011 Gala was announced in March, the show taking place on 24 May and to be broadcast on Channel 4 on 10 June. It was a who's who of the comedy world, with acts like Alan Carr, Michael McIntyre, Chris Moyles, Jack Dee, Dara O Briain, Jo Brand, John Bishop, Jonathan Ross, Rhod Gilbert, Sean Lock, Sarah Millican, Lee Evans, Jon Richardson and Jack Whitehall all taking part. And Micky Flanagan was also on the list, a nod of recognition as to how far he had come in the industry. He would now be playing in the O2 Arena alongside a line-up of household names. Quite rightly, he was excited yet nervous about the evening: the O2 holds a daunting 20,000 seats.

'Going up a gear in comedy is always a bit scarier whether you're going from a comedy club to a theatre or from a theatre to an arena – it's nerve wracking,' he told *Metro* in 2013. 'Otherwise you won't survive. I was nervous for the first few, now I really enjoy them because I've learned how to play them. It's the same show, just on a bigger scale. People ask if one man and a microphone can work in an arena but if it wasn't working, it would be empty. But they're coming in their droves. I don't see the problem.'

Filming the show was, essentially, an endurance event. The atmosphere was excitable but each comic had only a few minutes on stage to make his mark – and with an audience who had to sit through three and a half hours of filming, there was an air of expectancy.

There was also a spin-off show after the main event, which saw Dermot O'Leary backstage at the stand-up extravaganza hanging out to see who he would bump into, gate-crashing dressing rooms and having lunch and a gossip with the comedians to give viewers an inside track on what it was like performing in the biggest stand-up show ever.

Micky decided that such an occasion would need some short-sharp gags to give the patient audience what they deserved – unadulterated laughs. And that's just what he did. He started his seven-minute set by thanking his audience for travelling to the O2 on the London transport system. He then did his set about going to America and taking a girl out. But then he went on with some new material about how the only place he always liked going to was Spain, but he explained there was always an 'overwhelming fear of getting the shits'. It was then he told the audience about his travels to Mumbai for the opening weekend of The Comedy Store in India and the first thing he was warned about was getting the dreaded 'Delhi Belly'. The audience in the O2 were beginning to get an idea of what was coming and they were loving every minute. Micky continued the gag by shrugging off

the warnings, saying that he was acclimatised to such tummy troubles as he'd been going to Spain for years!

The joke carried on with Micky building up to the inevitable toilet humour.

'Day three and I don't feel right. I said to my mate Paul, "I'm a very regular man, I always go in the morning but it's half ten at night and I need to go." With the world's gentlest of pushes, the world fell out of my arse.'

The audience erupted; it was rude, crass and cheap but Micky's story-telling abilities and apparently genuine fear made it funny.

In the reviews that followed, Micky's name was mentioned several times as 'having one of the funniest sets of the night'. The *Independent* wrote that 'while videos from Miranda Hart and Whoopi Goldberg bombed, star turns came from Micky Flanagan and Sean Lock.' The *Telegraph* decided that 'Rhod Gilbert, Kevin Bishop and Micky Flanagan all acquitted themselves admirably,' while www.comedy.co.uk wrote: 'Flanagan's material was very strong and you could tell that he is a Comedy Store regular; in that he is able to deliver high quality sets for short spots. The audience loved him and he received one of the biggest rounds of applause of the night.'

And comedy website Chortle agreed. 'Micky Flanagan was another highlight of the night with a rather bottom-centric set, but the cheerily matter-of-fact way he described his bout of Delhi Belly proved a definite winner from this charismatic working-class everyman.'

And it wasn't to be the last time that Micky used the Delhi-belly sketch. He would later include it in his tour, Back in the Game, after satisfying himself that the audience appreciated a little risqué toilet humour.

On Friday, 17 June Micky's fans tuned in to watch him on David Walliams' new series, *Wall Of Fame*. It was the first time the show had been broadcast and it was billed as a cross between *A League Of Their Own* and *Mock The Week*. With David as the host and well-known household stars like comedian Jack Dee, socialite Tamara Ecclestone, Irish stand-up comedian Andrew Maxwell and *GM:TV* presenter Kate Garraway as the regular panelists, TV pundits thought it was the perfect show to air on a Friday night, as did Walliams.

'I'm looking forward to taking control of my new weekly, newsy, quizzy, gossipy, entertainment show,' the *Little Britain* star told Entertainment website Digital Spy. 'I will be taking my quizmaster role most seriously... with lots of laughter.'

Each week the regulars would be joined by two guests to complete each team of three and they would have to answer questions from rounds centred on a wall of the most talked-about faces of that week. It was broadcast on Sky1 and the guests for the first show were Micky and *X Factor* judge Tulisa Contostavlos. Micky was on Kate and Andrew's team and they triumphed, but sadly the series was not successful and was axed after just eight episodes.

During the summer months of July and August, Micky

had a bit of a well-earned break, and he told his Facebook fans he was looking forward to a proper summer holiday of doing 'proper f**k all'. But although he wasn't doing any tour dates, there were still television appearances to enjoy and on 15 July he made his first appearance on the popular panel show, *8 Out of 10 Cats*. Jimmy Carr is the host of the Channel 4 show that has been airing since 2005 and is based on statistics and opinion polls, asking a panel to guess the week's hot topics and results of the polls each round. Sean Lock and John Richardson were the team captains when Micky first appeared on the show in series 11, episode 5 (former team captains have been Dave Spikey and Jason Manford). Previous celebrity guests have included Alan Carr and David Walliams and filming took place at the BBC Television Centre, typically the day before transmission.

Micky was understandably nervous about the show. He has since spoken about how he finds TV appearances more daunting than his live shows, but he still took to Facebook to plug his debut. TV presenter Lorraine Kelly and Charlie Booker were on Jon's team while Micky found himself on Sean's team, alongside one of *The X Factor's* most notorious acts, Jedward. It was a baptism of fire for Micky; he was slightly over-shadowed by the double-act but if nothing else, he did look as if he was having a hilarious time as he spent most of it laughing at Jedward.

He got the audience and panel going with a story about

talking on the phone and how, as a child, he was brought up not to talk on the phone in case you incriminated yourself. Charlie Booker was astonished: 'You were told not to incriminate yourself as a child?' Lorraine Kelly couldn't work out why Micky was taught such a thing until he confessed that his dad was a bit of a bad lad. He concluded his tale with a warning from his mum. If he was talking on the phone and people were nearby listening, she would simply say, 'Earwigs at the rhubarb!' Micky explained this meant, 'Shut the f**k up'. The audience loved it, and so did the TV bosses as he was invited back on the show on 22 July but as he posted on his FB page, 'thankfully without Jedward!' The second episode saw him join Jon's team alongside Kelly Osbourne and go up against Jamelia and Jack Dee. He was back on the show at Christmas time, alongside Liza Tarbuck on Sean's team, competing against Greg Davis and those Irish boys again, Jedward, on Jon's team.

Micky would not be appearing at the Edinburgh Festival Fringe that year after having a break from his tour but for someone who had been to the Fringe (and got his big break from it), he still wanted to pay homage to the occasion.

'Good luck to all those with shows at this year's Festival,' he wrote on Facebook. 'But spare a thought for the good people of Edinburgh who for a whole month will not be able to get out of their turnings...' He was asked in a *GQ* interview the following year who he thought was

a misunderstood comedy genius from his years of seeing different acts at the EFF, but he politely replied that the word 'genius' is sometimes a little over-used in Edinburgh.

'It's a really tough one because if you go to the Edinburgh Festival, you'll find that every comic is a genius according to their flyer, so the actual word becomes devalued. In the end, you go, "I want to go and see the bloke who don't put 'genius' on his flyer or on his poster."'

In August he was on another TV show, *Chris Moyles' Quiz Night*, which aired on 12 August at 9.35pm on Channel 4. He encouraged his fans to tune in as he was starring alongside Dermot O'Leary and Barbara Windsor, who he described as 'proper East End royalty', and thoroughly enjoyed his experience. The show sees Chris act as the quizmaster while the three guest celebrities compete in a quiz about the week's events. Each star guest gets a chat with Chris first before taking part in the quiz, hoping to win the prize that Chris himself has donated. The loser has to sing out the show with the all-female house band.

When Micky joined Chris for a chat, the host wanted to know more about his career path and very cheekily pointed out that he'd been doing stand-up comedy since '1959'. He'd been a 25-year overnight success. Micky responded with, 'I don't like to rush things.' He then pondered whether he would make it on a show like *The Apprentice* as he hated Mondays so much, he wouldn't ever work – 'I would be fired but that would be a result,

I'd be down Wetherspoons.' He confessed to pleasuring himself during *Lark Rise To Candleford* as 'most men will either top themselves or have a w**k during a costume drama.' Even Moyles was a little aghast at his frankness. The quiz itself was a little nerve-wracking for Micky, who hated being put on the spot – and admitted that he was starting to sweat profusely as he was 'not a big fan of having to remember shit'.

But it wasn't just regular panel show appearances that Micky was picking up. In August it was announced that he would appear as the regular panelist on a new BBC1 gameshow called *Epic Win*. Filmed again at the BBC Television Studio and airing in the early evening slot on a Saturday night, the new family show was hosted by Alexander Armstrong and each week saw contestants complete individual challenges, such as trying to get dressed while bouncing a football. They then had the opportunity to win between £3 and £3,000 depending on what the panelists thought it was worth. It was a series that ran for six weeks and Micky was pleased that this was one of the first television shows that he would be able to watch with his son.

'Looking forward to finally watching a show I'm in with my little boy. But he's a harsh critic and we have to compete with *Ben 10* on the other side!' he told his Facebook fans.

The first episode aired on Saturday, 20 August and Micky was joined by Jason Manford and Nina Wadia.

For the next five weeks he was joined by two different celebrities, including Rita Simons and Katy Brand, Ed Byrne and Sunetra Sarker, Kevin Bridges and Alex Jones, Patrick Kielty, Stephen K Amos and Ann Widdecombe and finally, Jason Byrne and Joe Swash on the last show of the series, on 24 September.

Critics decided that the show was amusing enough for the early-evening family entertainment slot in the summer but it failed to take off and was cancelled after just one series. It wasn't too disappointing for Micky, though. He appeared on a new series of the immensely popular BBC series, *Shooting Stars*, on 12 September alongside Tamzin Outhwaite, Stone Roses legendary bassist Mani and comedy actor-turned-author Charlie Higson. Created and hosted by comedians Vic Reeves and Bob Mortimer, the panel show started its run in 1995 and although it follows a panel show format, the comics' slapstick and wacky humour often means that the rules are obeyed or forgotten about, depending on their mood. The guests often find themselves facing a surreal challenge set up by the guys at the end of the show. *Little Britain* star Matt Lucas had been the regular scorekeeper and dressed up as a big baby with a drum kit and called himself George Dawes. 'What's the score, George Dawes?' became a catchphrase for the show. He was replaced by Angelos Epithemiou.

It was a raucous affair but Micky got into the spirit of things quite quickly. He and Charlie joined regular team captain Ulrika Jonsson, while Jack Dee, the other team

captain, was joined by Tamzin and Mani. It was certainly a programme, broadcast at 10.35pm, that he would not be watching with his son but Micky made sure the fans knew about his appearance by posting a link on his Facebook page. Micky was becoming a regular face on the panel shows and not only this, he was at ease in the very different environments in which they worked. He even tried to do an American accent on *Shooting Stars*! Fellow comedian and actor John Thomson told entertainment website Digital Spy that panel shows are a 'closed shop' for comics with certain agencies but Micky was quick to point out that this was simply the 'business' side to showbusiness.

'It's not an accident that certain comedy agencies have a lot of great comics on their books. It's not a closed shop, it's a business,' he told Digital Spy. 'You've got to be careful about pointing the finger. The reason all those acts come from that single company is because that company gets the talented acts because it looks after them the best. That's just business. I get worried when comedians start trying to say that all we are is entertainers. We're not. We're in show business. Someone has to do the business and a good businessman will have the best people on his books.'

As well as making the point that it is the best people for the job who get booked, Micky has often spoken about the idea that the entertainment industry itself is a lot harder for those from a working-class background like himself to crack, whereas if he had middle-class family connections

in the industry the leap wouldn't seem so great. It was a topic he also discussed with Sean Lock for his *What Chance Change?* radio series.

'If you grow up in a very middle-class environment where your parents might work in the arts or in TV or music or something, it doesn't seem like that huge a leap for you to move into it. Growing up in a very working-class background, you have none of those connections. You don't feel as though it's your birthright to work in those industries. A lot of working-class kids, their only way out is whether they can sing, dance, play football or box. Working in the production of and making of a TV show or entertainment just seems like another world.'

Chapter 13

HE'S GOT THE
X FACTOR

'You measure your success by the people standing in front of you at a gig. When you start out playing to 20 people above a pub and then suddenly you're walking out at the Lyric Theatre to 1,000 people, that's special and that's your success.'
COMEDY CENTRAL WEBSITE

After his *Shooting Stars* appearance Micky had a couple of weeks' rest to prepare for his long stint at the Garrick Theatre, where he would be performing every night from Monday, 26 September to Saturday, 15 October 2011. The Garrick Theatre, named after one of the most prolific Shakespearean actors, David Garrick, seats 656. It is not one of the biggest venues that Micky has ever played but being sold out every night for 18 nights, it would be a consistent number. Micky had also made history with this run, as Nimax Theatres (who own the Garrick) confirmed

that his West End show was the fastest-selling stand-up ticket since Eddie Izzard's tour, over four years before. It was quite an achievement. Previous productions at the West End venue include *No Sex Please, We're British*, in 1982, *Mr and Mrs Nobody* with Judi Dench in 1986 and *One Flew Over The Cuckoo's Nest*, starring Christian Slater and Alex Kingston, in 2006. Now it was time for Micky to take his critically acclaimed Out Out show 'up west' for the run.

The *London Evening Standard* reviewer attended the press night, probably the most-feared evening by performers since it is the night when the media outlets from around the world gathered to watch and then offer their opinions on the show in their publications. But the *Standard* was positive:

> This gag-packed gig cemented Micky's star status. The woman next to me was heavily pregnant and I feared that she might go into labour as Flanagan triggered waves of hysteria with yarns that recalled his rise from ducker and diver to university educated household name. At times it seemed as if he could not quite believe his ongoing success story. A class act in every sense.

Micky made sure he added new material as well as the gags that he knew the audience were waiting for – his chicken children, the fancy-restaurant-ketchup gag and, of

course, the out out gag itself. And his fans could not have been happier: 'I had face-ache from laughing so much,' admitted BorrisB on the Ticketmaster website. 'We left the theatre with our jaw aching and two weeks later we are still quoting his jokes and lines,' confessed another. But it was the comments about the forthcoming DVD release that were exciting for Micky and his management. It wasn't due to be released until 14 November but already the hype was building among his fans. '2nd time I've seen him this year and was really impressed. Face was aching from all the laughing!! In fact, can't wait for the DVD to watch it all over and over again!' wrote jessydee. 'Love his style – down to earth and laugh out loud,' revealed JadeBilly. 'Will be getting the DVD to watch it again!'

Micky also built up the release of the DVD on his Facebook page, tempting his fans with photos of the artwork and posting links of how they could pre-order it. But with 20 more UK tour dates to get through before the release – he would finish his tour on the same day – he didn't have time to rest.

Five days after his final night at the Garrick, he travelled to Brighton to perform at the acclaimed Brighton Comedy Festival on 20 October. Running from Thursday, 13 October until 22 October, the BCF from the Brighton Dome was an event that welcomed a range of comics – from household names like Alan Carr and Michael McIntyre to those who had just got back from the Edinburgh Festival Fringe and were still perfecting their sets. Micky didn't

have time to see much of the action after he performed, though: he was in Wycombe at the Swan on Friday, 21 October and then took his tour to Ireland for the first time, playing in Dublin the following night at Vicar Street. He then moved to Belfast on the Sunday to appear at the Waterfront and then he was back in England the following day to play at the Lowry in Manchester. Thankfully, there was a day to rest before his next gig, which was in Leeds on 26 October, and then he was in Liverpool at the Empire on the 27th. October was whizzing by and Micky was on the final furlong of his tour but showing no signs of fatigue. He still managed to have a pint or two after a show although now it wasn't a quiet drink in the pub – after 40 years of cheerful anonymity, he was being recognised wherever he went.

'The bizarreness of it all is not so much strange people coming up to you, it's the strange places,' he told the *Telegraph* in 2013. 'I'm standing in the toilet and someone comes up to you and says, "Hello Micky! Are you all right? Shall we have a photo?" And I'll say, "Yes, but can we go into the bar and take it?" Don't get me wrong, I like talking to teenagers and it's nice when they come up and be like, "al-wight, Mick!" But I was in the local pub and knew I was firmly middle-aged when I looked at this bunch of teenagers and thought, "Just think, pull your trousers up, won't you?"'

Fans were still buying his tickets in droves and he had sold out 100 of his 160-date tour. Not only that but TV

bosses were keen to get Micky on board for his own TV show – although the format hadn't yet been decided. But he wasn't going to be happy with any old show, he wanted to make sure it was the right one for him. The *Independent* reported that he was in 'fierce negotiations' with several broadcasters to secure the right television show for his talents.

'Make no bones about it, unless I can make the show I want it's not going to happen,' he told the newspaper. 'I have my audience now, why would I want to make a s**t TV show and f**k that up?'

In October, it was announced by Channel 4 that they were commissioning a new panel show and Micky had agreed to be the regular team captain. The programme, due to be aired in 2012, was called *The Mad Bad Ad Show*, and featured Micky with two special guests going head-to-head with the other team captain, Mark Watson, while comedian Mark Dolan would host the show. A pilot was made earlier in the year and the channel decided that a series would be popular. Mark, along with Micky, had high hopes for the show.

'The format is a bit like a mixture of a quiz show and *The Apprentice*,' Micky told the British Comedy Guide website. 'I've been filming bits and pieces for it the past couple of days and I'm optimistic it is going to be entertaining fare. I don't think it will be too much like one of these panel shows where it's all fighty and I get depressed. It's going to be something a bit different. In a

good way. Not in the way that shows John Barrowman sing songs to deserving people is "something a bit different."'

The series, when it aired in February 2012 for six weeks, met with mixed reviews. 'While it was a chuckle it's not something I will be tuning in for every week,' wrote the TV reviewer for the *Shropshire Star*.

'If you enjoy the bits in-between the programmes better than the shows themselves then this one is for you,' wrote the *Daily Mirror* while the *Metro* wrote: 'There are all sorts of weirdness lurking in the depths of the ad industry and this new panel show exploits it to the full via quiz questions, challenges and banter. Cheeky cockney Micky Flanagan and self-deprecating Mark Watson are team captains.'

But www.comedy.co.uk wrote: 'It was brave of Channel 4 to try this rather "niche" twist on the ubiquitous panel show format, but it just didn't get on screen. The series certainly provided laughs and ticked a few geeky media/ TV trivia boxes but there was a real lack of purpose to the programme that ultimately made it feel hollow and stunted.'

There were some familiar guests on the line-up to add to its appeal – Jason Manford, Miles Jupp, Sean Lock, Lorraine Kelly, Rufus Hound and *Countdown* host Rachel Riley – all took part, but the programme was axed after one series by Channel 4.

At the end of October 2011, Micky made his way back to Scotland to play two more dates – one at the Edinburgh

Festival Theatre, which holds just under 2,000 seats, and the following day at Glasgow's King's Theatre, which has an audience capacity of 1,745 over four levels of seating. Micky joked that 'Nobody puts Micky in the corner!' when he came on stage, much to the audience's delight, in reference to his sharing the space with the Dirty Dancing set. The *Herald* went along to review the show and made a point of saying early on in the article how things had changed dramatically for the comic in comparison to the last time he was in Glasgow. They wrote:

> Micky Flanagan's last appearance in Glasgow attracted 22 people, so he's justifiably pleased to fill a theatre, strutting on stage to 'Saturday Night Fever'. There's a refreshing lack of modesty about a comic who brags about buying a £140 jumper yet refuses to pay 80p for a KitKat, after his career exploded following an appearance on the Royal Variety Performance. A keen observational eye, an assured sense of nostalgia and a turn of phrase that mixes his market trader and mature student vocabulary lets him survey the battle of the sexes and seems fresh.

With just 11 dates of his tour left to play, November was a blur of more travel and shows – Micky was in Reading on the 2nd, Blackburn on the 3rd and Newcastle on the 4th. It was on Friday, 4 November that he shared big news with his Facebook fans: he would be appearing on

BBC1's *Live At The Apollo* that evening but not just as an act, Micky would be the host for the evening, cementing his credentials as one of the country's most celebrated entertainers. Recorded weeks earlier, he had been asked to play host to the iconic show as it started its seventh series, and took to the stage to introduce two other comics – one of comedy's rising stars, Seann Walsh, and Irish favourite, Jason Byrne. The 9.30pm show got over 3 million viewers and Micky, in his normal low-key manner, told his Facebook fans that if they tuned in to watch, 'hopefully it will be the perfect antidote to the rain.'

With just 10 days of his tour left and the release of his DVD imminent, he had to mix his live stage performances in with publicity for the DVD, which meant taking part in various chat shows to promote it. After performing on stage at Ipswich and then Norwich, Watford and Guildford in early November, he headed to The London Studios on Thursday, 11 November to take part in the popular *Graham Norton Show*, a chat show that would be aired the following evening. Micky made his way into Studio 1 that night to be greeted by Graham and the assembled TV audience. It was the largest studio in the complex and depending on the size of the set, could accommodate audiences of over 600.

Micky was understandably nervous. Although he had appeared countless times on panel shows and quiz shows and was no stranger to the workings of a TV studio, this was his first televised interview and he would be chatting

to one of the country's most popular comedy interviewers, Graham Norton. Graham had been host to several chat shows in his TV career, including *So Graham Norton*, *The Graham Norton Effect*, and *The Graham Norton Show* and had won five BAFTAs. When *Friday Night With Jonathan Ross* came to an end in 2010, *The Graham Norton Show* was announced as the chat show that would be taking over the coveted Friday night slot, moving from its normal Monday night home.

Over the years, Graham had welcomed some of the biggest names in showbiz industry onto the sofa as guests, including Harrison Ford, Lady Gaga, Daniel Radcliffe, Paul McCartney, Robert De Niro, Elton John, Robbie Williams and Sylvester Stallone. And now it was Micky's turn. He would be making his debut appearance alongside Sir Cliff Richard, Lord Alan Sugar, and *X Factor* judge Kelly Rowland. It was, as he told his Facebook followers, 'quite the oddest bunch of people' he had ever sat down with.

Micky was first to be introduced for the night and came out smiling at the audience in a purple stripy shirt. Next up was Kelly, who sat in the middle and lastly, Sir Cliff Richard. Graham was dancing around while his guests shook hands and air-kissed, and Micky kept looking at the audience. The presenter made a point of telling Sir Cliff that he had been asking him for years to appear on his show but Cliff had always refused so he was delighted to finally have him on the sofa. He then turned to Micky

and said, 'And you, Micky, you've never been here before either, have you?' to which Micky replied, 'No, but I said yes straight away! No hesitation.'

Graham then quizzed him about being out on a Friday night (the show was recorded on Thursday but the guests would act as if it was going out live that Friday), to which Micky reeled off one of his other famous gags, about not remembering the last time he was out on a Friday, and how when he used to go out to a club he would hope the doorman would turn him away. It was a well-rehearsed gag but it worked. Graham then welcomed Kelly Rowland to the show and revealed that she would be performing her new single, 'Down For Whatever', at the end of the night and told the audience that there were 'backing dancers and everything'. Micky chipped in to say that he could be one of her backing dancers, to which Kelly replied, 'Yes, of course you can, as long as you can shake your booty.' Micky didn't need asking twice; he stood up, bent over and jiggled his bottom. Kelly loved it and Graham sat back in his chair, laughing his head off. It was only six minutes into the show and Micky had broken the ice. Graham spent a while talking to Cliff and Kelly about their showbiz careers and how they kept in shape before turning back to Micky.

'You are a man of a certain age, Micky... have you considered the gym?' Micky then puffed out his chest a bit and breathed in before saying, 'I'm not one of these men who go to the gym. I did go a couple of years ago.

I lay down on the mat to do some sit-ups and I woke up two hours later.'

It was a similar line to the one he told the audience in Mumbai but it got the audience laughing.

Lord Alan Sugar was then invited on to the show and was plugging his new autobiography. Graham picked up on the various gripes that he had in the book, one being the Italian restaurants in Florida not being vaguely Italian and making up their own Italian names for things. Micky stuck up his hand and talked about his latest trip to an Italian, where he asked for a Bruschetta. The Italian waiter told him off over his pronunciation and Micky turned around and said, 'Look mate, it's eight and a half quid for a bit of tomato on toast.' It was a joke that he had been using in some of his early comedy shows but Micky was on mainstream telly now and the audience loved it. Graham took the opportunity to plug the DVD and produced a copy to show the audience. He then told him he was like a 'pop star' as he had certain hits in his comedy routine that the fans wanted to hear. Graham asked him to perform his signature Out Out routine, or an abbreviated version of it for the guests, which Micky did. It got a tremendous round of applause and he looked chuffed. He also managed to slip in his gag about American ladies not understanding the Cockney accent, telling Kelly his story of going out with a girl and asking if he could come in her ''ouse'. Kelly was shocked, Graham was amused but Micky had managed to get four of his

well-crafted gags into a prime-time chat show. Not bad going at all!

But there were still three more dates to play and when Micky came to the final performance of his epic tour, Monday, 14 November at Derngate in Northampton, it was as much a relief as a sad occasion. His debut tour had sold out over 150 dates in 100 venues, helping him sell some 150,000 tickets. Just two years before he was a relative unknown but now he was one of the most popular comedians in the country. And now he had his DVD to plug, just in time for Christmas...

Chapter 14

HITTING THE TOP OF THE CHARTS

*'What am I doing next? I'm climbing Mount Kilimanjaro
and then I'm swimming the entire length of the Thames and
then I'm going to dig a hole to the centre of the Earth with a
toothpick. But I'll get that done over a weekend and I don't
know what I'll do on the Monday...'*

FEMALE FIRST, 2011

On 15 November 2011 Micky took part in an altogether different chat show, the popular ITV1 lunchtime show, *Loose Women*. The show features a panel of female presenters who interview celebrity guests and discuss topical issues. Micky wasn't an obvious choice of guest but after his success on Graham Norton, rubbing shoulders with four glamorous women was going to be right up his street. Sitting next to Carol McGiffin, Micky answered questions about his tour from anchor

host Andrea McLean, and from Lisa Maxwell and Jenny Éclair and thoroughly enjoyed being the focus of their attention. When asked about his DVD, he told the panel that although he had performed his Out Out skit in his 160-date tour, once it went to DVD he wouldn't be doing any of the material again.

'How would I describe the Out Out DVD? What you're getting is basically the greatest hits from the last 10 years of my stand-up. That's basically it. It was time to commit it to tape. I could never see any point in sending out a DVD that nobody would buy or watch,' he told the studio audience. 'I never saw the point in sending out all your best stuff recorded unless you have a fairly big market to send it out to, because you are sort of kissing it goodbye. The general rule is that once you've committed it to tape and people have bought it, you can't then perform it again live. And that's the one I'm sticking to.'

As well as being a good day in terms of his DVD promotion, Micky was also a little star-struck when he met a long-time hero of his, David Essex, who was also a guest on the show. He had been listening to David Essex songs when he was younger and it was a little strange now coming face to face with the singer, who had just had a part in the BBC1 soap *EastEnders*.

'I was star-struck. I just thought, "Blimey, you were a God when I was growing up,"' he told an interviewer for the *Radio Times*. But David Essex wasn't the only person who managed to make Micky feel a little tongue-tied.

After countless shows referring to having sex with his wife around *Grand Designs* and boiling rice, Micky was at a loss for words when he met the property show presenter, Kevin McCloud!

'I wasn't so much star-struck but just thought, "I've been watching you on the telly…" and just to be sitting there with him and I kept thinking, "Do not ask him the question he's probably been asked a million times, like what's your house like? What's your favourite type of window? How do you feel about mosaic tiles? He's like, "Oh shut up, I live in a caravan, it's all a ruse!"' Micky recalled to Female First.

Kevin McCloud and David Essex aren't the only two celebrities that Micky finds himself in a tizz over, though: he has a few female celebrity crushes too!

'I've got a terrible crush on Kirsty Wark,' he told the *Radio Times* in 2012. 'I have for a number of years. I've always had a thing for intellectual women slightly older than me; Joan Bakewell, Anna Raeburn and now Kirsty.'

At the beginning of December, sales of Micky's DVD were going well – he had gone straight into the main top 10 chart and was currently giving Peter Kay and his 'The Tour That Didn't Tour' a bit of competition in the charts. The *Telegraph* listed Micky's DVD as one of their Top 20 Stand-up comedy DVDs to get for Christmas, commenting, 'Something tells me that Flanagan – who feels like this year's big find even though he's been slogging away on the circuit for a while – will give Kay a run for his money,

although given that the latter had coined a reported £7m this year alone, he'll have to go a long way to match his bank balance.'

After three weeks on sale Micky's Out Out Tour DVD was number five in the charts, behind Alan Carr, John Bishop and Peter Kay. There was a surge of sales over Christmas and just a few weeks into the New Year, he hit the number one spot at the end of January 2012. He stayed at number one for several weeks and was over the moon at how well the DVD had sold, thanking his fans for their support whenever he had the opportunity.

'Hello one and all, I just wanted to say a massive thank you to everyone who has supported me this year and over the years, it's amazing and dare I say, at times, almost emotional!'

With his DVD riding high in the charts, there was plenty of time for other TV appearances before Christmas and having been touring for the last 14 months, Micky was now enjoying some free time from being on stage. But that didn't mean he wasn't in demand. TV shows wanted him to take part in their Christmas specials, including *Million Pound Drop*, *8 Out of 10 Cats*, *Argumental*, *Ruth Jones' Christmas Cracker* and *Home for the Holidays*. First up was Davina McCall's festive edition of *Million Pound Drop*, a game show in which two contestants are given £1 million pounds at the start of an eight-round game. Each round they answer a question with four possible answers and put their money on the answer they believe

to be correct. The answers all have trap doors on them so if it's the wrong answer they see their money fall through the trap door and they lose that amount. The aim is to try and get to the last round with £1 million but it's easier said than done!

Micky told his Facebook fans that he was busy 'swotting up' before his debut on the quiz show. He made sure to tell them to tune in at 10pm to C4 and wish him luck as he was playing for a very good cause.

He went on the show with his nephew Mike and they were the first pair of the evening. Davina introduced them as Micky and Mike and they met her on the podium to talk about the charity they were playing for, the Michael Sobell Hospice in Ruislip. Micky was understandably nervous – he had done very well on *Mastermind* but now there was the potential to win big money for their chosen charity and he wanted to do well. Speaking backstage he said: 'It is a lot of money to physically look at, it's nerve wracking in the respect that you are doing it for other people. And that level of responsibility is monumental.'

The pair got off to a good start and sailed through the first question with their million pounds and managed to get through several rounds with hundreds of thousands of pounds still in their possession but question four stumped them and they found that they had to split the money three ways as they weren't sure of the answer.

'You don't want to lose money but you have to realise that strategically you are going to lose money,' said Micky.

'But you have to try and lose the least money and that's what we did.'

They managed to make it through to the final round – a feat in itself for most contestants – and had just a bundle of £25k to play with. The question was: 'Which of these O'Connors has had more UK top twenty hit singles?' And Micky and Mike had to choose between Sinead O'Connor and Des O'Connor to put their cash on. They chose Des and after an agonising wait, it was revealed to be the correct answer and so they were able to give the Michael Sobell Hospice £25k.

'We're over the moon about winning the money for the Hospice,' Micky said afterwards.

Micky was back on the radio on 10 December, this time taking part in Clive Anderson's Radio 4 show, *Loose Ends*. The programme brings together an eclectic mix of comedians, actors and musical sessions. Micky chatted about his working-class upbringing, plugged his DVD and featured in the same episode as one of his comedy heroes, Monty Python legend Eric Idle. He had always been heavily influenced by the Monty Python comedy group since a young boy, when he and his dad would watch them on TV in their show, *Monty Python's Flying Circus*, making this a surreal yet poignant moment for him.

There was further good news for the comedian in December when the nominees for the British Comedy Awards 2011 were announced on Sunday, 11 December. Micky's agent rang him with the exciting news that he

had been nominated in the Best Breakthrough Comedy Artist category, a category that celebrates some of the best new comedians in the public eye that year. Micky was overwhelmed that he'd been nominated. Previous winners included John Bishop, Charlie Brooker, Simon Bird and James Corden. Micky told his fans that he was 'Absolutely delighted to have been nominated for a British Comedy Award!'

The awards were held at Fountain Studios in North London and to mark the occasion, Micky took Cathy along. It was the first time on the red carpet for both of them – although it was blue for the Comedy awards – and when they arrived at the bash, they stood and posed in front of the cameras, with Micky putting a protective arm around his wife. Cathy, dressed in a gorgeous midnight blue cowl dress and black Jimmy Choo shoes looked every inch the star herself, if not a little nervous as the hordes of photographers who had gathered for the event shouted at them to pose and smile in their direction. But she held on to Micky, who was also suitably suited and booted for the occasion in a black suit and black tie and joked to the paparazzi that he'd splashed on the Paco Rabanne.

Micky made sure he signed a few autographs for the fans who had braved the chilly December evening before he and Cathy made their way inside, where they mingled with the likes of Miranda Hart, Hugh Dennis, Harry Hill, Graham Norton, Rob Brydon, Jack Whitehall and Alan Carr. As well as the biggest names in comedy, the event

also attracted mainstream celebrities too and Hollywood A-lister Goldie Hawn, Oscar winner Helen Mirren, boxer Amir Khan, Freddie Star, McFly, the cast of *The Only Way Is Essex*, the cast of *Made In Chelsea*, Jerry Hall and pop princess Kylie Minogue were all in attendance.

Jonathan Ross was the host and took to the stage to start the proceedings after the guests had enjoyed the selection of fantastic canapés on offer, including Thai Tiger prawns with sweet chilli glaze, Rosemary lamb fillet on minted polenta cakes and Mozzarella and sundried tomato tartlet with olive tapenade, washed down with glasses of Champagne and Champagne cocktails. The event was being broadcast live on Channel 4, and Wossy made sure he got off to a typically outrageous start when he recapped the year's comic highlights with a series of typically risqué jokes, including reference to the on-going Leveson Inquiry into media ethics, suggesting it should be renamed *Would I Lie to You?*

The winner of Micky's award was due to be announced later in the evening and the tension built as the winners of the other categories were announced and celebrated. After Jonathan Ross announced the winner of The Best TV Comedy Actress, which was presented to Miranda Hart for her sitcom *Miranda* – she told the audience she couldn't wait to get home, put the kettle on and get into her onesie – it was time for the winner of the Best Comedy Breakthrough Artist to be announced. Micky had been nominated for his performance at the Royal Variety

Performance and was up against Greg Davis in *Ask Rhod Gilbert*, Tom Rosenthal from *Friday Night Dinner* and Dan Skinner, for his character Angelos Epithemiou. He was feeling confident as the video clips of his hugely successful stint at the RVP played but in the end it was Dan's name that was read out as the winner and Micky, who smiled graciously as the cameras panned to the losers in the category, still went away with the honour of being nominated. He could at least consol himself with the fact that most of his loyal supporters and fans thought he had been robbed!

'Can't believe @mickyFlanagan didn't win! Funniest bloke alive!' wrote @ksmithprop on Twitter, while @sazzysue wrote 'FFS! MickyF should have won! Get out out Mick! #robbed.'

But Micky had enjoyed the experience and the night wasn't a total disaster; he was able to let his curly locks down with Cath and enjoy the 'ambience'. But there was one uncomfortable moment for him, though – he doesn't like any politician to try and be 'cool'!

'I get very uncomfortable whenever I see politicians trying to be hip or funny. They wheeled out Vince Cable at the British Comedy Awards; it's like wheeling me out at the UN.'

TV work continued as Christmas drew nearer. The next was a guest appearance on *Ruth Jones' Christmas Cracker*, a seasonal chat show packed full of celebrity interviews, musical performances and other fun and games.

Welsh actress and comedy star Ruth Jones had first found fame in the popular series, *Gavin & Stacey*, having co-written the show with her friend, James Corden. The pair have since gone on to enjoy much success with various television shows and presenting gigs and Micky was excited to be asked to come on the show, only the third *Christmas Cracker* that Ruth had presented, to talk about his DVD. Being on a chatshow wasn't as daunting for Micky any more – in fact, larking about in front of a live studio audience and mixing with different celebrities was something of a treat for him now, and he made sure he played up to the audience in style.

On the show, which was broadcast on BBC2 on Wednesday, 21 December at 10pm, Micky appeared alongside singing sensation Lulu, The Manic Street Preachers and James Corden. Dressed in a flowery shirt and dark jeans, he decided to showcase his now infamous 'cockney walk' to Ruth and James and the studio audience. He jumped off the sofa and paraded about in front of the stage, first demonstrating his 'casual cockney' strut, building up to his 'under-threat' cockney walk before doing his final 'can't hang abaaat' quick cockney stride. Ruth and James cackled away and the audience enjoyed it. The skit had been a crowd pleaser since he first performed it years ago and it was still getting the same amount of laughs now as it did then.

Micky made sure his Facebook fans were kept up-to-date with his various TV appearances too and also made

sure they knew when to catch him on the box. He appeared on Channel 4's *Home for the Holidays: Extra Stuffing* show, a spin-off to Vernon Kay's *Home for the Holidays* show that gave viewers the chance to interact with the guests. Hosted by comedian Charlie Baker, he told Micky that he had a special present for him, the fortune-telling fish, which he had to hold in his hand. The cameras then cut to Charlie, dressed head to toe in a red fish suit and with the prediction that Micky would have a 'passionate' year. Micky looked bemused, 'I better stay at home, give 'er indoors a nudge on New Year's Day and say, "come on babe, the fish never lies,"' he told a laughing Charlie.

There were two more TV appearances before he could be at home with ''er indoors' and Max, firstly *Argumental*, Dave's hit panel show that sees two teams of comedians argue over various topical issues. Sean Lock was the host with Robert Webb and Seann Walsh team captains and in this festive edition of the show, on 22 December, Micky was a guest alongside Jason Manford. He took great pleasure in arguing that Santa is better than Jesus. It was typical tongue-in-cheek Micky humour and there were the perfect rude yet laugh-out-loud gags for the show. He knew how to tone down his potential offensiveness or play up to it, depending on the situation. For instance, the swear words from his mouth on this show would have had some of the 'Loose Women' audience blushing for England!

On 23 December Micky was at home with the family

but as *8 Out of 10 Cats* had been pre-recorded earlier that week, he was also on the box taking part in a festive edition of the quiz show. Once again he guest-starred on Sean's team, alongside Liza Tarbuck, and he was competing against his old foes, Jedward, who, along with Greg Davis, made up Jon's team. It might have been two days away from Christmas but he wasn't going to go soft on the boys. He had witnessed their childish (some might say annoying) antics on the show the first time round but his confidence levels and TV experience had come a long way since then and he wasn't afraid to speak his mind. Dressed in identical bright green sparkly jackets, the twins were a prime target and when they interrupted one of his jokes, Micky called them 'dickheads', much to the shock and then amusement of the studio audience and Jimmy Carr. In their defence Jedward didn't seem to realise what was going on.

For Micky 2011 had been a year of tours, TV appearances and terrific experiences and there was more to come. Knowing that he had to 'strike while the iron was hot', he was already working on his next line of stand-up gigs for 2012, where the country would see and enjoy more of him and his everyman humour. But he had some important business to attend to before all that, telling Female First online that there was no rest for the wicked.

'What's next for me? I'm climbing Mount Kilamanjaro and then I'm swimming the entire length of the Thames

and then I'm going to dig a hole to the centre of the Earth with a toothpick. But I'll get that done over a weekend and I don't know what I'll do on the Monday. Probably watch *The Wright Stuff* with a cup of tea!' joked Micky when talking to the Female First website in 2011.

Chapter 15

A LEAGUE OF
HIS OWN

'I was asked to do I'm A Celebrity... Get Me Out Of Here!
and I jokingly said to my agent, "I'd rather eat my own shit."
"You'd be perfect!" they said, "you'd walk it!"'
RADIO TIMES, 2012

If 2011 was a year that catapulted Micky to nationwide
fame, 2012 was going to confirm his newfound
household name status. He had been working solidly
the past 15 months and you could forgive him if, at the
beginning of 2012, he wanted a little breathing space. But
no, that wasn't his style. However popular his tour or
however well his DVD had sold, Micky hadn't forgotten
his roots – or more importantly, the countless jobs he did
as a youngster to earn a wage or the 15 years he had spent
honing his comedy act.

'If you're a working-class kid who's done a day's work

on a building site for £50, then you're on stage doing 20 minutes of something you really enjoy and someone pays you double for that – that's when I cracked it, as far as I was concerned,' Micky admitted to the *Radio Times* in 2012.

But being famous wasn't something he ever took for granted either. He knew he was and he enjoyed the comfortable lifestyle it gave him and his family but he wasn't ever blasé about his level of fame.

'I still have all my decorating tools down in my cellar, all my paintbrushes and all my guns,' he told the *Telegraph* in 2013. 'Sometimes if the phone doesn't ring for a couple of days, I say to my wife, don't worry, I've got the paintbrushes downstairs. I know full well that if this all went tits up tomorrow I would be making money by this time next week painting and decorating.'

Fame, however much it wasn't changing him per se, was changing the way people around him acted and he found himself the target of random strangers just wanting to talk to him. To a man who was used to blending in, this was something he sometimes had to endure through gritted teeth. But Micky is a people person and he found it fascinating that folk such as teachers and social workers would be the ones coming up to him telling him they wouldn't be able to do what he did – i.e. stand up on the stage and tell jokes – in a million years.

'Success changes the way people talk to you. I've had the same conversation over a thousand times the past year

or so, people come up to you and go, "Mick, Mick, can I tell you something? I could never do your job in a million years, did you know that? I could never do your job." And I don't know exactly what to say to that but I'm thinking, "Well that's cos you're a bit boring, aren't you?" People with proper jobs say this to me, the teachers, the social workers, the people holding this mess together; they are the ones saying this to me. A man said this to me the other day and I asked him what he did for a living. He told me he was a brain surgeon.'

There was no taking a break for Micky in 2012; he was already back on the stage at the Soho Theatre with His 'Work in Progress' shows. The Work in Progress shows are performed by comedians who are in between tours or gearing up for a new nationwide tour; by playing smaller pubs and clubs they are able to try out new material and sketches to gauge what works and what doesn't in front of a live audience – who in turn get to watch a top-class comedian perform without paying for a full-priced tour ticket.

Michael McIntyre caused a little controversy with his Work in Progress shows later that year when he announced that he would be playing several nights at the Edinburgh Festival Fringe as he was preparing for a new tour and critics thought it was out of order that he was charging over £30 for a ticket to watch 'half-complete jokes, unfinished silly dances and ill-fitting Morningside accents'. Nevertheless, these shows received consistently

positive reviews, and offered McIntyre the opportunity to hone his act prior to launching the official tour.

Micky's Work in Progress shows were a chance for him to keep his name abroad on the comedy circuit and he made sure there were plenty of opportunities for his fans to watch him perform live, first at the Soho Theatre (he also went back there by popular demand in June for extra dates), The Monday Club in The Tattershall Castle in February and then the Pleasance Theatre in Islington and The Boat Show in March (and again later in May for more sell-out shows).

As well as working on his stage shows and perfecting his jokes, the TV work was still coming in – but there were certain invitations that he wasn't ever going to accept. When ITV1 asked his agent if he would consider taking part in their jungle reality show, *I'm A Celebrity… Get Me Out Of Here!* that year, he flatly refused. Being in the jungle among a bunch of other celebrities, taking part in 'bush tucker' trials that included lying in a box of cockroaches or eating Kangaroo testicles was not for him.

But there were shows that Micky would gladly accept being part of, including the previously mentioned *The Mad Bad Ad Show*, which began airing on 17 February (it only ran for one series). Then Micky joined Kevin Bridges for an episode of his *What's The Story?* series, which aired on Wednesday, 15 February at 10.45pm on BBC1. Kevin launches his own advertising campaign for

the city of Glasgow, gets a voice-coaching lesson and wins over people down south who could not understand his thick Scottish accent. And he spent time with Micky to talk about accents and all things comedic. Micky had Kevin in stitches when he recalled a time when he was working as a busboy in America, where he would be in charge of making tea and coffee for the customers. He explained that the milk that Americans would ask for is called Half and Half (half cream and half milk). For Cockney Micky, this was pronounced ''arf and 'arf' and he retold the joke about asking a customer who was with one diner who had already made the order, if they wanted ''arf and 'arf 'n' all?' It was a joke he had made on the *Graham Norton Show* the previous year but it was relevant to Kevin's suggestion about whether he was tired of being referred to as the 'Cockney Comic' while he regularly got 'the jock'.

Speaking of America, at the beginning of March Micky travelled to New York to take part in *The Secret Policeman's Ball*. Started 36 years ago by Amnesty International and Monty Python star John Cleese, they gathered comics from across the globe for a gala to raise funds for the human rights organisation. The last *Secret Policeman's Ball* was in London four years before and it made its American debut in 2012 at New York's Radio City Music Hall. The 180-minute show, which was later shown on Channel 4 on Friday, 9 March at 10pm, had an impressive range of stars performing for the charity,

including Russell Brand, Liam Neeson, Ben Stiller, Kristen Wiig, Seth Meyers, The Muppets, Eddie Izzard and Jack Whitehall. Micky told his Facebook fans how 'honoured' he was to be part of the show, which also included performances from Mumford & Sons and Coldplay, who happily announced that they 'take pleasure in being the least funny act here.'

Micky decided to perform his sketch about why the teenage pregnancy rate is so high. He talked through his opinions on it being due to the lost art of 'fingering' and the audience, although not altogether sure how to respond at first, did titter quietly and Micky carried on happily with the gag. He thought it was a 'great show, we did our greatest hits for a fantastic cause,' and persuaded his fans to watch the show when it aired on Channel 4.

In March he also took part in Frank Skinner's series, *Room 101*, a show that invites three celebrity guests on each week to tell Frank their biggest gripes. Frank then decides which moan is worthy of being sent to 'Room 101', gone forever. Micky, being Micky, had several good gripes he wanted to get off his chest. He was on the show with politician John Prescott and actress Rebecca Front.

One of his moans was celebrity chefs and their 'over-valued idea of cooking'. Up came a picture of Gordon Ramsay on a mocked-up cover of a celebrity magazine and Micky launched into his spiel about why he doesn't like them.

'All they've done is get organised, that's it, they've got

the time and they get organised. Gordon Ramsay is always angry and I know why cos he's doing a woman's job,' he told Frank on *Room 101*.

It was part impromptu gripe and part well-rehearsed gag from his previous shows and Frank agreed with him, making Micky's day when they were banished into Room 101.

Later in the month the excitement of the new tour was building momentum. At the beginning of April he was planning the publicity around his tour and took part in a photo shoot for images that would accompany the tour. His fans were keen to offer their suggestions about what sort of photos – and they ranged from the ridiculous to well-thought-out dress-up costumes that represented some of his best gags.

'Why not dress up in a giant tomato ketchup bottle and stand in the middle of a busy restaurant?' suggested one. 'Do a photo shoot of you with five beautiful women carrying you and make it known that one is a transvestite. Will get people talking and wondering,' said another. 'Why not mirror David Beckham's H&M advert and stuff a load of socks down your undies. Except instead of white y-fronts you could wear paisley patterned briefs!' another fan suggested.

The suggestions were endless and Micky thanked all his fans for their input. But he didn't give them the information they were desperate for – when was the next tour going to be and what would it be called?

Instead, he continued to plug his 'Work in Progress' shows and it was only at the beginning of May that his followers finally got the news they were desperate for – there was a teaser about Micky's 2013 tour and if they clicked on a link on Facebook they would receive exclusive details about the show and be able to find out about access to tickets before anyone else. That was the first time, on 2 May, that he appealed directly to his fans about his tour. The publicity posters that accompanied his many posts over the next few days were of him pointing to the camera, again encouraging them to sign up on his website to be part of the gang that would get exclusive information about the tour before anyone else.

In May he appeared in James Corden's popular sporting panel show, *A League of Their Own*, which had retired cricketer Freddie Flintoff and former England football midfielder Jamie Redknapp as team captains and comedian Jack Whitehall as a regular team member on Freddie's team. A cross between *A Question of Sport* and a sports related comedy show, James mixed jokes with sports stars, welcoming some of the high profile athletes from the UK and top stars in the world of football, cricket, rugby, tennis, athletics and motor-sport alongside some of the biggest names in comedy. The mixture of high jinks and seeing some household names lark about on the weekly physical challenges made for great Friday evening entertainment, and for Micky, it was a chance to have fun and act like a big kid. Something that would come very easily!

Filmed at London's Elstree studios, Micky was taking part on Jamie's team alongside Gabby Logan and Olympic athlete Jessica Ennis was participating on Freddie and Jack's team. Micky joked that the episode 'showed off his athleticism... The London Olympics loss is comedy's gain!' and although his team was beaten 8–6, it showed Micky to be a good sport and he was invited back on to the show twice more. It was also the first time that he had met sports presenter Gabby Logan and they struck up a friendly banter after the show – Micky was very impressed that she had attempted to drink a pint of 'tripe smoothie' as one of the challenges for the episode but more impressively, when he and Jack Whitehall went head-to-head in the physical challenge, Micky won! Not bad for a middle-aged geezer.

Gabby was famous for presenting *Final Score* for BBC Sport and co-hosting *Sports Personality of the Year* and while the pair got on well, neither Gabby or Micky could have predicted that just a year later they would be appearing on their own series together, *I Love My Country*, as host and team captain respectively.

Micky put his comedy skills to good use once more when he took part in Channel 4's *Comedy Gala*, again at the O2. In aid of Great Ormond Street Hospital, the event didn't seem as daunting for him after his success on the previous year's show. Filmed on 11 May and aired on Channel 4 on the 20th, pop star and judge/vocal coach on BBC1's new talent show, *The Voice UK*, Jessie J opened

the show and Micky was 13th in the line-up (unlucky for some) behind Alan Carr, Jack Dee, Keith Lemon, Jonathan Ross, Paul Chowdhry, Michael McIntyre, Jimeóin, Josh Widdicombe, Sean Walsh, Jack Whitehall and Andi Osho. The reviews were much the same as the previous year with Micky's apparent ease in the huge arena just one of the reasons why several critics and audience members put him top of their 'favourite acts of the night' list.

May continued to be the build-up for the tour and Micky made sure his fans got regular updates on what was happening – on the 16th the announcement came that the UK and Ireland tour was confirmed and tickets for Micky's Back in the Game tour were due to go on sale that Friday at 9am. A short promo video of Micky accompanied the advert and on Friday it was all systems go as sales for his second nationwide tour started selling out. Originally scheduled to run over 50 dates from 7 February 2013 to 25 May, it was obvious after just 5 days that Micky's second tour was going to be as successful – if not more – than his first sell-out tour so organisers started adding extra dates to the scheduled run. A further 13 days were added to the diary across the country, including further dates at Wembley and The O2.

The ticket sales were going through the roof: over a quarter of a million were sold in the first week and at the beginning of June it was announced that another further 5 dates had been added – including another 3 at the O2 Arena as he had sold out 4 already. Three more Wembley

arena dates were added and Micky found that his pre-planned finish date had been re-scheduled for 6 months later – with all the extra dates added, his tour would wrap on Saturday, 23 November at Birmingham National Indoor Arena.

The *Telegraph* reported that Micky was 'on course to sell more than half a million tickets on this tour, making it the biggest stand-up tour of the year.' But preparing for a tour on such a scale was no walk in the park. Micky was no stranger to hard work and he continued to do his Work in Progress shows up and down the country to test what worked and what didn't in front of an audience. If the last tour was about how he had gone from a working-class kid to a middle-aged intellectual, this show was more about where he was now – having the odd mid-life crisis, living in East Dulwich with his wife and six-year-old son.

'It's a move forward now from the last show, more or less setting me right in the time and place I am now as a fifty-year-old man living in a leafy middle-class suburb. It's bringing the story right up to date and ultimately reflecting on the past and how things have changed, which my audience tends to really like,' Micky explained to the *Telegraph* in 2013. 'It's about keeping the zest and fun in your life as you get older. I don't like this creeping ageism in the world.'

And like it they did. The Work in Progress tour was selling out, as were tickets for his Back in the Game tour, especially for the big arenas, which Micky himself

admitted wouldn't have happened 20 years earlier as there just wasn't the same demand for stand-up comedy. It gets a lot more television exposure and that has really created the industry and demand for the arena gigs and the DVDs. But selling out such shows wasn't as simple as writing a few gags, road-testing them on a smaller audience and then believing you had a 'show'. For Micky, it was all about preparation and making sure he struck a chord with his audience. He would spend over 100 hours writing for the new show and that would get him to the point where he would be ready to perform on stage. But of course, like any performance, the element of actually 'performing' the material was the essential bit. A lot of Micky's act was then honed depending on how the audience would react to certain gags. It was an evolving process and he was always adapting it to get it right. In an interview with the *Telegraph* in 2013, he revealed:

'The element of surprise in comedy is still very important. There's a bit of an unwritten rule that once you have committed something to DVD that you don't perform it live to them again. The live experience is different. I can remember smoky rooms above pubs, in front of 10 people – three of them had paid to get in, two were getting out of the rain. I remember that clearly. That's why I'm always working.'

With the tour shaping up, it was inevitable that the audience would be looking for some of the same popular, repeatable gags that made his Out Out tour so successful.

The Ketchup story, the chicken children and of course, the popping out out gag itself. Those classic routines couldn't be repeated but they had to be matched and Micky was busy preparing what he thought would reach the standard of his debut tour. And this one was about the small things in life that he enjoys, as he told the *Portsmouth News* in 2013.

'The centrepiece is about me making a sausage sandwich. My life has slowed down to such a point if my wife goes out for the day that's how I create excitement. I also talk about the two off-licences in my life – the one I go to normally and the one I pop into for the second bottle of wine. Things like that. So all these details I'm pulling in to say, "This is where I'm at now."'

At the beginning of June he was back on one of his favourite shows, *8 Out of 10 Cats*, this time alongside new presenter Krishnan Guru-Murthy on Sean's team. They were playing against *Strictly Come Dancing* presenter Tess Daly and Hari Kondabolu, an Indian-American comic. They lost the episodes 1–4 but he was back on the series three weeks later, this time on Jon's team alongside dancer Louie Spence. This was one of the most watched episodes of the show because host Jimmy Carr had been in the public eye over a tax avoidance scheme and the BBC entertainment website reported that viewing figures peaked at 2.7 million, compared to the average viewing figures of 1.3 million. Almost half of the 45-minute show was taken up by jibes from the panel at Jimmy's expense

and, knowing what he was letting himself in for, he introduced the show with 'Welcome to *8 Out of 10 Cats*, a show about opinion polls, statistics and I'm guessing, this week, me!'

Sean, who had Geordie comic Sarah Millican and TV presenter Georgie Thompson on his team, made sure he got the first dig in by commenting, 'We all like to put a bit of money away for a rainy day, Jimmy. But you're more prepared than Noah!' Micky, meanwhile, after Jon's comedy rant brightened the mood by asking, 'Can I have that £15 you owe me?'

While his new tour tickets were selling like hot cakes, Micky made sure he also promoted the release of the audio CD version of his Out Out tour. 'You can listen to it in the car when you can't get out the turnin'!' he wrote on Facebook.

On Wednesday, 13 June, a new Channel 4 series, *A Short History of Everything Else*, was broadcast, with host Griff Rhys Jones presiding over team captains Marcus Brigstocke and Charlie Baker and guests over their shared experiences of the past 30 years. It was an alternative view of social history and along with archive footage, the team captains and their guests tried to prove that they could remember more about 'everything else' than the other team, adding their own irreverent interpretations along the way. There was only one comedian who fitted the bill of society historian – and that was Micky, who was asked to take part in the very first episode of the show, alongside

Kirsty Wark. Never one to be tongue-tied, Micky was a little embarrassed at meeting the newsreader, having previously spoken of his long-standing crush on her in the *Radio Times* in February. The show didn't receive many positive reviews from critics, with some of them pointing out that Micky had taken on the 'Alan Davis' role of ditzy panelist, while Kirsty was the intellectual heavyweight.

The following evening Micky fans could watch him take part on *Mock The Week* again, this time as a guest on Andy's team alongside fellow comedian Nathan Caton in the first episode of the new series. Micky was taking over the television – whatever show you tuned in to it seemed, you could watch him, which was ironic as at the start of 2012, he had planned to give himself a bit of a break – simply doing the Work in Progress shows and working on material for the new tour. But TV bosses weren't in on that plan and in just 6 months he had clocked up 8 TV appearances – not to mention the bucketload of festive appearances in the run-up to Christmas the previous year. The rest of the year continued in a similar vein, with appearances on *The Big Fat Quiz of the 80s*, *Live at the Apollo*, *8 Out of 10 Cats* again and a new show, *I Love My Country*. In an interview the following year, he told a journalist that he himself was beginning to get a bit sick of the sight of his mug on the telly, too.

'I was starting to think I'd have to start watching foreign TV to avoid myself!' he joked.

His latest TV appearance, on *Live at the Apollo* on 21

July, was a repeat from his November 2011 show and some fans didn't realise it wasn't a new episode, prompting them to complain that, 'watching *Live at the Apollo* was like watching your DVD. Bit disappointed really. New material would have been good.'

But there was a treat in store for fans who hadn't yet bought his Out Out tour DVD. It was due to be shown on Saturday, 18 August on Channel 4 and Micky, for one, wanted people to tune in as he had his pride at stake – 'I don't want to be beaten by *Casualty*!' he explained. As the summer months continued, more dates were being added for his Back in the Game tour, the latest addition being two new dates in Scotland, one more in April at the Edinburgh Playhouse and one in October at the new Hydro Arena in Glasgow.

The second tour was growing by the month but Micky was undaunted, he had a job to do. He might not be as young as some of the whippersnapper comics on the scene but that was part of his charm. And talking of age, there was a very important birthday to celebrate on 11 October 2012: Micky was about to turn half a century...

Chapter 16

MASTER(CHEF) AT FIFTY

*'I can't nick things any more. These are the problems
of being successful. A sandwich here, a chocolate bar there.
Apparently crime and success don't go hand in hand!'*
INTERVIEW WITH GRAHAM NORTON

Turning fifty years of age for some men would indicate a more relaxed pace to life, but not Micky. He was about to embark on a gruelling nationwide tour as well as fulfil his many TV commitments and start to pen his autobiography... There was no slowing down for him. He had a quiet celebration with his wife and family to celebrity the big day but made no bones about it being a milestone birthday. Hitting the big 5-0 can sometimes be quite daunting for a man. This is the time for a midlife crisis, a time of reflection and a time of panic and self-doubt – what have I achieved in 50 years? For Micky

though, who was using all his experience of hitting middle age in his stand-up show, turning fifty wasn't just about what he'd done, it was about what else was on the cards for him.

'I wanted to be a spokesman for people in middle age to say you are still in the game,' he told a journalist for the *Sheffield Star*. 'I'm still going "out, out" but it's less and less because it takes days to recover from a late night now, but I don't like this creeping ageism in the world where the only people who are exciting or having any fun are twenty-year-olds.' Micky, more than many fifty-year-olds, was, as the saying goes, living the dream in terms of his career. But like anyone reaching that point in his life, it made him evaluate his life too.

'Hitting 50 affected me more than I thought it would,' he told *The Star*. 'There's no running away from the fact you've lived a great big chunk of your life. You would have to be a fairly dense person not to start taking that on board. There's a sense of urgency to get on with things and get things done that you want to do.'

Society doesn't help those over a certain age either; there is a sense of being 'past it' in the entertainment industry long before any evidence to support such a claim. But with so many young, talented stars making their way into the spotlight, suddenly being cast aside for someone younger than him was a real threat. And Micky, who had taken years to get to this point, wasn't going to give up his microphone easily. That wasn't to say other people didn't

have an opinion about a fifty-year-old stand-up, however. 'Someone suggested I should lie about my age,' he revealed in a 2010 interview in the *Guardian*. 'If I was a film star or a pop star maybe, but comedians are supposed to tell the truth. Frankie Boyle says you can't be a stand-up after 40. On the other hand, Bob Monkhouse once said you can't be funny until you are over 40. So how much time does that leave you to be funny? About a year.'

But while the media industry didn't always openly favour people over a certain age, as long as Micky was at the top of his game, he believed he would succeed for years to come.

Delivering the goods was something that he never failed to do. It was also one of the reasons he was constantly booked by TV bosses to appear on their programmes. His latest project was to be part of the team involved in Channel 4's Stand Up to Cancer campaign. Channel 4 had joined forces with Cancer Research UK to launch the fundraising initiative, Stand Up to Cancer UK, to help accelerate ground-breaking research into curing cancer. A range of stars and celebrities from the worlds of film, music, TV and comedy all joined the fundraising evening on Friday, 19 October 2012 to raise awareness and funds for the charity. Davina McCall, Alan Carr and Dr Christian Jessen hosted the evening and welcomed some of the biggest stars in the UK and America, including Bradley Cooper, Leona Lewis, Cheryl Cole, Heidi Klum, Jeremy Piven, Alesha Dixon, Dawn O'Porter, Jonathan Ross,

Jack Whitehall and Max Beesley to the show. There was a special high stakes game of *The Million Pound Drop* with the Harry Potter cast, Tom Felton and Warwick Davis, the cast from *8 Out of 10 Cats* had a special episode and Alan Carr welcomed an array of special guests to his extra-special *Chatty Man* show.

Throughout the night there were top-class musical performances and skits involving comedians and celebs doing unusual things. The cast of *Made in Chelsea* worked in Tesco, for example. Micky took part in his own special sketch that saw him invited up to the BT Tower to see how the telephone lines were playing such an important part in the fundraising extravaganza. It was a tongue-in-cheek video that saw him getting up to mischief by chatting to one of the big bosses in charge and comically pressing the 'do not touch' button which then disconnected all the phone lines across Britain. In the end the connections were restored and Micky just carried on as normal. 'Don't sweat the small stuff, fella!' he told the boss before doing his cockney walk out of shot.

But that wasn't the only appearance from Micky that evening: he was a specially invited guest onto Alan Carr's special *Chatty Man* edition and shared the sofa alongside Gok Wan, actress Anna Friel and Bear Grylls. Alan told Micky that L'Oréal should 'forget about Cheryl Cole' and work with him – 'I was looking at the back of your head earlier and it's got tremendous volume.' Micky then admitted to using a volumiser although Gok

quickly pointed out that it was a 'diffuser', much to the amusement of the studio audience. Alan then gave all the guests a special Stand Up to Cancer t-shirt to model for the evening, with Micky struggling to put his on as he thought Alan had deliberately given him a smaller size. Alan then introduced supermodel Heidi Klum to show the guests how to model the t-shirts properly. Micky was a good sport throughout and with his help (and the other celebrities) raised over £8 million for the good cause.

A League Of Their Own came calling twice again in November for Micky. On 16 November he appeared with Jessica Ennis as a guest on Jamie's side and went up against Jimmy Carr, who was with Freddie and Jack. It was a bit of an embarrassing show for Micky as he took part in a challenge that required him to step into the ring with two female wrestlers. He appeared very cocky at first, and after slipping into a pair of tiny trunks to take on The Blossom Twins for the 'quick fire round', he told the studio audience that he was used to the tiny outfit as that is how he 'dresses up every night for the wife'. But the cheeky smile was quickly wiped off his face when he begged for mercy after being held in a chokehold. He did, however, manage to last a little longer than Jack and the rivalry between them increased. At the end of the month, he appeared again on the show with Zara Phillips on Jamie's team and was up against Laura Trott on Freddie and Jack's team. Taking part in the physical challenge again, he and Jack donned their Lycra cycling gear and

competed in an uphill cycle challenge. Again, it was close between them but Micky came up trumps. Would Jack ever triumph over Micky?

The extra TV exposure for Micky was one of the reasons why extra performances kept being added to his tour. There were announcements in October that additional dates had been added to London, Dublin and Belfast arenas as well as new shows in Birmingham and Bournemouth. Sales of his Work in Progress shows were also selling out and more dates were announced for those shows, including the Leicester Square Theatre from 6 to 27 November.

As well as promoting the tour, Micky let slip that in 2013 he would be taking part in a brand-new gameshow commissioned by BBC1 and due to air in August the following year. Micky told his Facebook followers that they were in with a chance to be in the audience for the show if they followed a link – and they would get priority seating if they contacted the production company via email.

It seemed like it was non-stop for the fifty-year-old comic and 2013 was going to be even more full-on when the Back in the Game tour started on 7 February. There was some other good news at the end of 2012 as he was named *The Sun*'s Comedian of the Year 2012. He might not have scooped the British Comedy Awards gong but this was just as noteworthy for the comic. He had featured in their Best of 2011 list, alongside Sarah Millican and Alan Carr. The tabloid's comedy editor, Tommy Holgate,

revealed that 'Micky sits high up on the list simply due to the nature of his tour extensions.'

In January 2013 he was invited onto *The Jonathan Ross Show* to chat about his upcoming tour where he sat alongside Paloma Faith and American actor Jamie Foxx in the Green Room before being welcomed out by Wossy. When Jonathan's BBC show, *Friday Night with Jonathan Ross*, finished in 2010, he signed a new contract with ITV and started a new chat show on a Saturday night. He was still pulling in the A-list guests although towards the end of 2012, he bemoaned the fact that his ratings were dropping due to the poor selection of guests, speculating that more mega-stars preferred the relaxed atmosphere of *The Graham Norton Show*.

Dressed in a plum coloured shirt, Micky waved to the audience before telling Jonathan that he was 'double busy' because of the tour so he was happy to be there 'as long as it didn't go on too long.' He was still doing some preparatory shows, the Work in Progress shows, he said, which needed just a few more bits of tweaking before the proper tour began, the following month.

It was a jokey, tongue-in-cheek interview and gave Micky a chance to recount some tales from his East End childhood. But he did admit that there was no chance of him ever getting a big head when he went home to visit his parents (who still lived in the same area) or his old mates – they would spot him walking down the Bethnal Green road and shout out 'Flanagan! W**ker!'

Wossy then asked him about his energy levels now he had reached a certain age and whether he had had to make any lifestyle changes to keep up with the demands of touring.

'Naaa, I'm doing anything,' shrugged Mick. 'You gotta remember, Jon, I am of the generation who partied hard, cocaine, ecstasy, and I'm not worried. I haven't gone crazy. I have got a tattoo though, I have my pin number under my ball bag.'

It wasn't the only show he did before the tour kicked off. He was invited onto *The One Show* to chat about his Out Out DVD and the upcoming Back in the Game shows and sat on the sofa alongside Fleetwood Mac's Mick Fleetwood. Unusually for Micky, it was an experience that he later told entertainment.ie made him feel very nervous.

'I don't get stage fright but whenever new things come up I obviously feel the nerves associated with that. Certain TV events make me nervous, anything live on TV. I did *The One Show* recently and I was very nervous, just trying to think of something to say. Actual stage fright no, but it wouldn't be human not to feel nervous. It's part of your job though. If you don't want to put yourself in this position then don't. I don't remember the last time somebody pushed me on stage with a cattle prod. I've elected to do it.'

The One Show is a daily live magazine-style show, hosted by Alex Jones, Matt Baker and Chris Evans, and showcases stories from around the country as well

as inviting celebrity guests into the studio. For someone who performs live on a nightly basis to large crowds it was unusual for Micky to admit that he does get nervous out of his comfort zone but it was testament to his professionalism that it didn't stop him fulfilling his promotional duties.

As well as taking part in many charity fundraising events, Micky was invited to take part in Comic Relief 2013, in a *MasterChef* special in March. Comic Relief holds a fundraising extravaganza every 2 years and encourages people to donate by 'doing something funny for money'. It was celebrating its 25th year.

The show, which attracted some of the biggest stars in the showbiz world to perform, do sketches, dance and generally make fools of themselves in order to raise funds, also featured special episodes of some of the well-known TV shows. The cast of *EastEnders* often did a musical number, while the stars of *Strictly Come Dancing* also performed special dances. *MasterChef*, the popular cookery show starring John Torode and Greg Wallace, also got involved and invited two celebrities to go head-to-head in a battle to raise a few laughs and hopefully, a lot of money.

So, on 15 March, that is exactly what Micky Flanagan and Jack Whitehall did. They went up against each other in the kitchen to impress the judges and be crowned *MasterChef* champion. The stand-ups were cooking in the kitchen of London's Australian Embassy and were preparing meals for Aussie icon Dame Edna

Everage, Australia High Commissioner Mike Rann and *MasterChef* judges Monica Galetti and Gregg Wallace. The narrator announced that Micky would be making a starter consisting of ham, eggs and pork crackling and the fish course, John Dory with red wine sauce and fruit accompaniment.

'One of my biggest fears about coming into the world of cookery is that I would go straight to the top very quickly,' Micky deadpanned to the camera. 'I'm not pleased with the way my dish turned out, but I'm pleased I got all my timings right and I put in all the ingredients that I said I'd put in.'

Dame Edna was one of the toughest judges the show had ever seen and decided that Micky's dish didn't 'justify the death of a fish', crowning Jack Whitehall the winner. He thanked his mother for 'providing all of his recipes' and rejoiced in the fact that he had finally triumphed over Micky.

The TV work didn't overshadow the important business of the new tour, however, and on 7 February Micky performed for a sell-out crowd at the Chatham Central Hall on the first date of his Back in the Game tour. This was it, time to hit the road once more and travel the length and breadth of the country to entertain... Look out UK, Micky was Back in the Game...

Chapter 17

PROUD PORK PIE
THIEF

*'So, the downside to all my success? I'm not allowed
to steal anymore. I've been stealing at a low level most of
my adult life, I like stealing sandwiches. Up and down the
motorway, the cost of the sandwiches was ridiculous
and I thought, I'm not having it.'*

Out Out, 2013

'Look! Look what I got, Barry, look! I got a couple of mini pork pies away. Result! One each, Baz, I'm not greedy....' Micky waited until the audience's laughter died down. He was telling the story of him pilfering a few pork pies from the motorway service station, much to the horror of his tour manager, Barry. It was typical Micky: not afraid to show a naughty side and that even though he was famous, he still liked to nick the odd thing to keep some level of excitement in his life. He carried on

the tale by insisting that his manager was shocked by his theft, asking Micky why on earth – with his life going so well for him at the moment – he would want to go to jail for stealing.

The crowd at the Central Chatham Theatre loved it. It was all part of Micky's new set – the revelation that he, a successful middle-aged man, is admitting to being a bit of tea-leaf and 'gets a quick kick out of stealing small things, like sandwiches. I've been stealing them for about 15 years. But when I had a bit of success I was called in by the promoter and he sat me down and we had a bit of a meeting. He said, "We've heard a little bit of a whisper that you steal sandwiches when you're on the road." I had to front it out, didn't I? The promoter told me we had a problem. He said, "The problem is, we can't have a couple of thousand people waiting to see ya and you're nicking a sandwich. We'll have to give everyone their money back, the insurance people won't pay out. Do you see our problem?"'

The audiences up and down the country loved it. Only Micky was so openly honest about every area of his life – and was being honest about being dishonest. Not that he sees the problem with nicking the odd thing or two – even now.

'I see it as levelling the playing field because everything is so expensive,' he told a bemused Graham Norton when he appeared back on his show in June that year. 'They make you pack your own shopping at Tesco. I don't

remember applying for a job. Why am I working here? So if you get a packet of crisps and you put them in really gently, they don't always show up. I don't do it as much now as I used to – I can't cos I'm the bloke off the telly!'

The opening night of his tour was a stormer. The tour advice was that the show was only suitable for over-fourteen-year-olds and probably most suited for over-sixteens only. Micky might have appeared on many family-friendly TV shows but his live tours pulled no punches – telling a vicar he was gay, just to see the reaction when he said he was tired after tea-bagging his boyfriend was just one example. For those appreciating the London lad's brand of rude humour, he wasn't about to disappoint. After the opening night of the tour he headed to Hastings, Tunbridge Wells, Dorking, Reading and Basingstoke, where a reviewer from the *Telegraph* wrote:

Few comics combine the gift of the gab with a facility for theoretical insight; fewer still can wrap sophisticated distinctions in to a catchphrase. Here was someone raised on the East End council estate plainly blessed with the common touch and an uncommon intellectual savvy – a real breath of fresh air. Back in the Game delivers the goods laugh-wise and it doesn't matter that it's not up there with Out Out, but if Flanagan's having to go quite so far back for grabby material then the question arises: has he

got enough of what it takes up his sleeve to stay the course? That said, it is sold out, sold out, sold out. If you want to see his new touring show this spring then you can pretty much forget it. And you'd better get scrambling for tickets when it resumes on an arena scale in the autumn.

Micky's schedule was full-on but with Barry driving him from gig to gig in what Micky loved calling his 'flash motor', getting himself to different venues on time and driving through the night was a distant memory. February was a busy time: he visited Northampton, Coventry, High Wycombe, St Albans, Portsmouth and Watford. On 23 February he was in Southampton, before having a few nights' break before heading back to Southend-on-Sea again, for two nights' performance at Southend Cliffs Pavilion.

There was a bit of a break in March, mainly due to Comic Relief and other TV commitments, like taking part in the British *GQ* Comedy Special. He did an in-depth interview with the upmarket lads' mag and also featured in the trailer for the edition, posing in front of the cameras on a council estate in a smart black suit in the rain. After introducing the special edition, he walks off out of shot moaning about the 'pissing rain' and a piano drops down from above, crashing onto the very spot where Micky was standing.

Website Chortle published a review of his show at the end of March and decided that although Micky was

lacking some of the laughs from his Out Out tour, he hadn't lost his common touch to appeal to the audience, even though his was 'a famous comic, earning a small fortune selling out big theatres and soon arenas.'

This follow-up to the breakthrough tour contained nothing as magnificently crafted and performed as either his trademark 'out out' routine or the delightful description of dining out at a swanky restaurant with its carefully cultivated 'ombayance' but it still proved Micky is a bit tasty when it comes to the stand-up game. That's down to two almost indefinable, intrinsic things: the distinctive rhythms and contorted vowels of the Cockney patois and his mischievous attitude towards sneaking an easy life through a series of small victories – both of which play into a hardwired British stereotype of blokes from his part of the capital. But it's on the co-existence of men and women that Flanagan has the most to say. It risks sliding into cliché but just about avoids it simply by dint of the situations he describes seeming so familiar to anyone in a relationship. The 'Back in The Game' [is] a reference to the big story of the show, and the relationship [with] his wife.

Micky himself addressed the critics' view about whether people still asked him to do Out Out in an interview after a gig in Sheffield. He did admit that he was happy to

perform it every now and again, but felt he was cheating the audience with it. Even though the interviewer suggests that at one point, the crowd would 'throw shoes at him to get him to do it, they wanted it that much!'

'It [the Out Out gag] does come out once in a blue moon if the audience drive me crazy. But as a comedian, you have to retain that you are in charge,' Micky explained to the *Bristol Press* in 2013. 'I've learnt over the years that the audience might want it but they know it so well, they don't laugh as much. The element of surprise in comedy is such an important thing.'

In April he was still tweaking and re-working some aspects of his show. There were still areas with room for improvement, he decided, in certain sketches and ultimately, he didn't want to disappoint his fans. This was very important to him. He admitted he was ultimately 'trying to keep up with how big he [had] got,' and his attitude hadn't changed from when he was performing in front of just a handful of punters, over 10 years before: Give them a good show and make them laugh. And laugh they did. He performed sell-out shows that month in York at the Barbican, for two nights at the Edinburgh Playhouse and then the Aberdeen Music Hall and Dundee's Caird Hall. Then it was time to travel for nightly shows in Blackburn, Sheffield, Belfast, Preston, Peterborough and Lincoln, before heading to Nottingham and Wolverhampton and then four consecutive nights at Bristol's Colston Hall from 24–27 April. The Bristol

dates were all sell-outs and he had to add a further date in September to keep up with demand from Bristolians who couldn't get enough of him.

According to the *Bristol Post*

Micky Flanagan is on top of his game right now. He's riding the crest of the zeitgeist comedy wave, his massive UK tour is breaking all manner of records and for the fourth consecutive night his one-man stand-up show packed the Colston Hall. The tone is most certainly adult and the language was correspondingly colourful but for the best part of two hours he had the crowd roaring with laughter. Mrs Flanagan is a rich source of material and stories of his own son popped in and out too, emphasising that no topic, however close to home, was off limits. A terrifically funny man and a great evening out.

There was one last date to play in April, at Oxford's New Theatre, before heading to Liverpool, Middlesbrough, Newcastle, Glasgow and Carlisle in May.

The nightly shows were hard-going; Micky had a longer set to perform that also included a short interval to give himself (and his audience) a breather. No one was getting short-changed from Micky and he was proud that he was giving his fans plenty of value for money. The *Telegraph* reported on his on-going sell-out success by stating, 'His live tour is on course to sell more than

half a million tickets – making it the biggest stand-up tour of the year.'

With tickets for his tour in such demand, it was probably no surprise that some people decided to forego a night with Micky and cash in on his popularity instead, selling their tickets on eBay to make a tidy profit. One set of tickets (two seated together with unrestricted view) for the performance at the De Montfort Hall in Leicester on 22 May, which on face value cost £22.50 each, sold for double that at £81. It had over 10 bids on it and fans were prepared to pay over the odds to get their hands on the chance to watch Micky perform live. The same happened when someone posted two tickets on eBay for his show at the Hackney Empire, which were bought originally for £28 each. They eventually sold, after 5 bids, for a whopping £104. Not only were people scrambling to get tickets, his fans were not averse to travelling great distances to see him either – one couple wrote on Micky's Facebook wall that they had travelled all the way from Alicante in Spain just to see his show for the evening. Now that's what you call popping 'out, out!'

The rest of May was a whirlwind, with shows in Warrington, Halifax, the Manchester Apollo, Blackpool Opera House, Cymru Llandudno in Wales and Leicester.

In between the touring Micky had spare moments to take part in interviews and talk about the subjects in his new show. It was becoming clear that although his wife was getting a raw deal from his material, his son, by and

large, was being left alone. And there was one very good reason for that, as Micky explained.

'My son is at an age now where he watches, listens and takes it all in. If I am going to talk about him, I'll ask him first,' he told the *Portsmouth News* in 2013. 'He has to go to school and he is getting to the point where he will see me on *The One Show* and he'll go, "Why did you say that?" So I make it more general rather than say it is specifically about him. I imagine in a few years' time he'll use it as a negotiating tactic. I'll only be allowed to make jokes about him if he gets a new bike.'

He also told *GQ Magazine* that talking about his son might not be appealing to as much of the audience as his wife jokes, namely because a lot of his fans don't always want to hear children gags, 'if they're not parents'.

'Whenever I'm trying to talk about my little boy, I always find that bit quite tough, because as a parent what you find funny absolutely falls on deaf ears. So that's why you have to come up with a joke so non-parents can laugh at the frustration of it.'

On 21 May it was time to get back to London to perform at the Croydon Fairfield Halls, then two nights at the Hammersmith Apollo followed by two nights at the New Wimbledon Theatre. The tour was originally meant to end in May but there was no chance of that happening. Micky's big arena tour was coming up in the autumn and punctuating that were shows in some of the smaller venues that were part of the added extra dates

to keep up with popular demand. On 30 and 31 May he played at the London Hackney Empire and it was the place he had decided to record his DVD.

'The geezer's geezer plays two triumphant dates on his home turf, east London,' said the website www. londonisfunny.com. 'There's only two things I know about women – they love a new top and they love talking,' Flanagan told the packed Empire. They loved it, and rewarded him with gales of laughter and screams.

Micky told his audience in Hackney that he was pleased he had chosen Hackney as the place for his DVD recording. There was none of the heckling there had been with the first one but then his venues were larger than his debut tour. Not that he couldn't cope with the odd heckler or two, but the Hackney crowd were all about appreciating one of their own. And Micky appreciated that.

'Ladies and gentlemen, when we had a meeting to talk about the DVD, loads of options came up and I said it could only be one place, The 'Ackney Empire,' he told the cheering crowd. 'I said the audience won't let us down and I was correct, you have been brilliant. Thank you!'

He walked off stage to the theme tune, 'Get Here' by Oleta Adams, with a cheeky wave and came back on for several encores. That was it, it was the end of the spring tour, and Micky was elated. The feedback was incredible, he had won rave reviews from every corner of the press, from *The Times* to the *Daily Star*, and he had sold out

more than 100 venues and still had an autumn full of arena performances to play.

But before those big-time shows, it was time to get back in the TV studios and the following month, on 7 June, he took part in *The Graham Norton Show* once again. Fresh from his tour but not yet ready for a rest, Graham introduced Micky as his 'favourite comedian in all the land!' He was on the show with *Downton Abbey* star Dan Stevens and the American star of supernatural TV drama *Heroes* Hayden Panettiere. Micky was dressed in a smart grey suit and black shirt.

Graham told the audience that Micky was back on tour in September and read out some of the big arenas that he would be visiting.

'Seven nights at the O2? That's just nuts, Micky! It's brilliant, but nuts! And three at Wembley!'

'These venues are enormous,' Micky told a somewhat baffled Hayden Panettiere. 'The O2 holds 12,000 people for stand-up.'

'You have no stage fright?' she asked.

'No, not really – I'd be in a bit of trouble if I did,' he said.

Graham then went on to talk about the tour and some of the things he didn't know about Micky that were revealed in the show, namely his love of stealing. Dan came up with some suggestions too about how best to put things through on the self-checkout without being caught and Graham told him people were going to 'watch him like a

hawk!' to which Micky retorted, 'Yeah, but that adds to the frisson!'

Micky then cheekily told Dan that he'd love to see a scene on *Downton* that involved all the men getting pissed in the wine cellar before Lady Mary comes down and they say to her, 'F**k off and get your own dinner!' Dan and the audience thought it was hilarious and Dan said to Micky, 'Watch out in series five!'

Micky was finding it hard not to stare at Hayden's boobs, which he readily admitted to Graham – who revealed he and Dan had been struggling too. So when Graham asked about the tattoo that was written down her back and obscured by her top, Micky jokingly chided the audience as to why they weren't shouting, 'Off, off, off!' 'Very un-British of you all,' he said.

Micky enjoyed joking with both the guests, making Hayden put on her best cockney voice and try out for a bit part in *EastEnders* by mimicking him saying, 'Get aat of my pub!' He then took the micky out of Dan and *Downton Abbey*, saying it was ladies' television.

'My wife loves it, sadly. If you have a bloke who cuddles up on the sofa with you with some wine and chocolates and *Downton Abbey*, he's a homosexual.'

And he didn't stop there. Pharrell Williams and Robin Thicke were on the show, performing their new hit single, 'Blurred Lines', and Rapper Pharrell was in his signature look – no socks, rolled-up trousers and smart shoes. So when they came to the sofa after their performance

there was only one thing Micky could do. He crossed his legs and showed off his own rolled-up trouser and bare legs, having taken his socks off in the musical interlude. Pharrell didn't seem that impressed.

The same night that Micky was entertaining on Graham Norton's show was also the Friday that tickets went on sale for 5 extra dates for the autumn leg of his tour. He had sold nearly half a million tickets already and, as mentioned on Graham Norton, would take in an impressive 7 shows at the O2 in London (having already sold out 4) plus 3 at Wembley Arena before it all finished on 23 November at Birmingham's National Indoor Arena.

With summer in full swing, it was time for Micky to take some well-deserved time off and holiday with his family. He planned a couple of weeks in Spain to rest and then told website jongleurs.com that he had agreed to take his son camping too, but he wasn't looking forward to it that much.

'It'll be hell from beginning to end, but I do it for him because his mates are going. They'll all be off enjoying themselves while I'm left on my own, pumping up the airbed, going "This is fatherhood." I have moments, like a lot of fathers from working-class backgrounds, of realising how lucky he is and how different his life is from mine. But then I think: good. He lives a very nice life, full of activity and fun and friends and security. It's small beer that he's not allowed to roam the streets and play on bomb debris.'

In August Micky was one of the stars in the new celebrity gameshow, *I Love My Country*. It featured Micky and Frank Skinner as team captains, sports presenter Gabby Logan as host and two celebrity guests would be joining each captain each week. Popstar Jamelia was the resident singer for musical interludes throughout the show and the studio audience was split in two to sit behind each team as the supporting crowd.

It was a contest to see which team knew their country best, featuring geography rounds and knowledge of the British Isles, and welcomed a range of celebrities from the worlds of music, sport and comedy, including Susanna Reid, Tom Ellis, Christine Bleakley, Dame Kelly Holmes, Martine McCutcheon, Rachel Riley, Rebecca Adlington, Sara Cox, Natalie Cassidy, Peter Shilton, Alex Jones, Martin Kemp, Iwan Thomas and Eamonn Holmes. Micky was very excited about the concept. Here was a Saturday night show that heralded the return of good old-fashioned family entertainment TV, a show that could be enjoyed by people of all ages.

'Too often I put on Saturday night TV and it's always someone trying to sing their way out of the ghetto – "If I don't get this, Nanna won't get her new knees" – or it's celebrities ceaselessly promoting themselves,' Micky told TV magazine, *What's On TV*, in 2013. 'I just want to do a show where people can put it on and you can sit down with the three generations – Nan, Mum and Dad and the kids – and everyone can have a laugh at different bits.'

Micky was a patriot and was keen to point out that other countries had issues a lot greater than ours.

'You've only got to come back from most countries to see that their problems are more brutal than ours,' he continued. 'Feels like we've been trying to put things right for a couple of hundred years. It's up and down but we're trying in this country to be democratic and fair and good.'

Being in charge of a team of celebrities with a screaming audience behind him, Micky was in his element. His geography wasn't brilliant but when former *EastEnder* actress, Martine McCutcheon came on the show and told him that she loved him because 'even my husband said I was allowed to fancy you,' she made up for that failing.

Micky loved it – he was able to indulge his devilish side and it featured all sorts of ridiculous special rounds. The national gurning champion, for example, judged the teams as they gurned individually and to the hilarity of the crowd, Micky won. He also managed to win 7 out of the 8 shows of the series, not only showcasing his ability to entertain as a team captain and keep the audience in fits of giggles with his one-liners, but he wasn't actually hopeless at geography either! Sadly, while it did make for light-hearted family viewing, the critics and TV bosses didn't agree and decided to pull the plug, meaning it only ran for just 1 series of 8 episodes due to the poor ratings – averaging a disappointing 2.8 million viewers over the series.

'The whole thing is as stiffly formatted but soggy-

bottomed and unappealing as an Iceland ready-made that's been left out of the freezer,' wrote the *Independent*, while the *Guardian* was even more ruthless:

> *I Love My Country*: idiot TV at its worst. What would you get if you crossed a UKIP rally and *A Question Of Sport*? Probably something like this jingoistic mess. In a year that has brought us atrocities such as *Splash!* and *The Voice* and *Britain's Brightest* and *Your Face Sounds Familiar*, *I Love My Country* stands out as being almost unsurpassably terrible. It's not even terrible in an entertaining way, it just makes you feel sad for everyone involved.

But Micky wasn't so impressed by the decision and told Digital Spy website that it was a shame it was axed so prematurely.

'Some people loved it, others weren't so keen but that's the nature of true art. I enjoyed the show. It reclaimed Saturday night TV for the family and took it away from people who think they can change their lives by singing a song.'

He also revealed that it was in fact a brave decision to do a brand-new gameshow format and put it in the middle of the summer months – it was actually filmed before Christmas in 2012.

'Those Saturday night shows aren't easy to get right but I thought it was a brave effort. Showbusiness is a

serious business and you have to take it seriously. What is presented is a lot of fun, and it was, but it does take hard work too.'

Speaking of hard work, as August drifted by in a summer haze, September crept up and heralded a fresh start for those returning to school. For Micky, it was the same sort of feeling, as he told his fans on 3 September it was 'soon time to go back to school, sorry, back on the road, 6 September, Ipswich, here I come.'

Micky was Back in the Game and back on the road...

Chapter 18

BACK IN THE GAME

'This is a serious business and you have to take it seriously.
It takes a lot of hard work to get right.'
METRO, 2013

On 6 September 2013 Micky was back on stage. He had nightly performances for the next two days in Ipswich Regent Theatre before heading to Plymouth Pavilions for two nights on 8 and 13 September.

Then he was off to Bristol (the 14th) before hitting Norwich Theatre Royal for three nights (19, 20, 21) and two sell-out nights in Hull's City Hall (24 and 25). The rest of the month featured shows in Newcastle Metro Arena on 26 September, Leeds Arena on the 27th and Sheffield Motorpoint Arena on Saturday, the 28th.

At the beginning of October he was back on the box as well as being on stage when he started filming a new Channel

4 panel show called *Was It Something I Said?* The show was hosted by David Mitchell and two teams, captained by Micky and Richard Ayoade, were pitted against each other in a battle of wordplay, answering questions based on quotations, tweets and autobiographies as well as the teams' very own one-liners to test their verbal mettle.

The first episode was broadcast on Sunday, 6 October and Jimmy Carr and Charlie Higson were the guests on the teams, as well as *Homeland* star David Harewood as the guest narrator. It ran for 8 episodes and Micky won 2 shows, drawing 2. The celebrity guests that appeared on the show included Ed Byrne, Gabby Logan, Jason Manford, Bob Mortimer, Robert Webb, Miles Jupp, Reginald D. Hunter, Sally Phillips, Rhod Gilbert, Josie Long, Josh Widdicombe and Vic Reeves. Reviews were mixed, with the *Radio Times* deciding it was 'worth a look' while several critics pointed out the few number of women on the show was particularly disappointing.

'The rhythms of the game itself are still a bit halting (it's early days) but the guests are funny enough that it barely matters – when Micky Flanagan impersonated David Mitchell being a bailiff, it's almost as if we're watching *Would I Lie To You?* – and in this genre there is no higher compliment,' wrote the *Radio Times*.

Micky was hopeful that series 2 would be permitted as he enjoyed the programme tremendously, but mostly the warm-up bits before the show started when he could chat openly with the guests about his thoughts... one being

how much he loved a 'zip-up cardigan'. This was what Micky did best – take control of the audience and the guests and be himself. He loved it. And so did his fans!

But back to his tour, and on 2 October he played Portsmouth Guildhall before moving on to Wembley Arena for his 3 sold-out nights on 3, 4 and 5 October. Located right next to Wembley stadium, Wembley Arena has a capacity of over 12,000, making it the second largest venue after London's O2. The *Evening Standard* gave the show 5 stars and described Micky as being firmly in the 'superstar bracket. Not that you would think it by his blokey opening in which he suggests he is going to sign off "after Christmas." Nothing revolutionary, simply mainstream humour at its best, the comedic equivalent of Flanagan's favourite radio station, Magic FM. Call it Magic MF.'

After his stint in London it was time to fly up to Scotland to perform at Aberdeen's AECC, before hitting Glasgow to play at The Hydro. The Hydro, which only opened officially on 30 September that year with a special concert by Rod Stewart, holds 12,000 people and tickets to see Micky's performance were just £24.50 including fees. Like playing at the O2, Micky was calm about the prospect, telling the *Daily Record* that he treats every capacious venue the same – he tries to make it an intimate, communal experience:

Everyone has an opinion about comedy stepping up to this size of venue, and ultimately you can only

put the tickets on sale, you can't force people to buy them. If you want to see the show in an arena, you can. They're aware of the size, they're aware of the screens. I've sat in audiences at gigs that size and all I've seen is smiling faces. Your performance is the same as if you were in a small theatre, but your performance is on this massive screen. People need to be able to see your face and expressions for comedy. It means even with the worst seat in the house, you can still see the geezer on the stage.

Micky's show impressed the crowds wherever he played. As well as making the big arena 'intimate', he was selling out the slightly smaller ones without leaving anyone to feel as though they were getting a poor deal. It was widely accepted that while there were no stand-out gags like his Out Out or restaurant ones from the previous tour, there were enough smaller jokes in there to keep the set ticking along nicely. There was a lot about dogs in the show, from suggesting that things in this country have become such that we are now servants to our four-legged friends – 'We follow them around and pick up their shit, they've got this sussed!' – to meeting a new girlfriend and being horrified that she let the dog lick her face goodbye, 'and as he's doing it he's looking at you, thinking, "Oh yeah, who's in charge now, eh son?"'

After The Hydro it was time to head to Belfast the following day to play at the O2 and then on Wednesday,

16 October he began his first stint at the O2 Arena in London, playing three nights from 16 to 19 October. Oasis star Noel Gallagher was just one of the famous faces in the audience and he called it a 'brilliant, brilliant show.'

Sadly for Micky, the high of performing at the O2 wasn't a feeling that was going to last long. On Tuesday, 22 October, his management team made the sad announcement that Micky would be postponing 4 of his next shows due to the death of his beloved mother, Sylvie. As someone who had featured on his radio show, his Out Out DVD and in endless gags in his shows, the audience felt like they were also losing someone they knew well and expressed sympathy for Micky and his family.

Micky hadn't made the decision to cancel his shows lightly but as a professional comedian, playing a half-hearted show was never on the agenda. He, as a son who had lost his mum, needed time to grieve and to spend time with his dad and siblings to come to terms with their loss. The message from his management could not have been clearer and his fans were left in no doubt that although the upcoming shows were postponed they would still see Micky in action, just two months later than originally planned. The official announcement, which was picked up in all the media outlets, from BBC's *Newsbeat* to the *Daily Express*, read:

Micky Flanagan has taken the difficult decision to postpone his forthcoming shows at The Brighton

Centre on 23 October and The O2 Arena on 24, 25 & 26 October 2013 following the sad loss of his mother. The Brighton Centre date has been rescheduled to the 7th of December and The O2 Arena dates have been rescheduled to the 2, 3 & 4 December 2013 respectively. If you are unable to attend the rescheduled dates, please return your ticket to the point of purchase prior to November 15 2013 for a refund.

Micky and his team were doing all they could to keep the fans happy and when he walked onto the stage at Bournemouth International Centre on Wednesday, 30 October, the audience made sure he felt especially welcome with an extra-big cheer and a standing ovation at the end. Knowing the show must go on, he performed without anyone questioning whether he was in the right frame of mind and had the audiences in stitches with his pork-pie stealing stories. With just one more England date left to play in October, Thursday, 31 at Cardiff Motorpoint Arena (which had been sold out for months), Micky was, in his own words, Back in the Game.

At the beginning of November he had three nights at Cardiff Motorpoint Arena to play (1st to the 3rd) and he was welcomed with open arms to the Welsh capital. Then it was three nights break before he headed to Sheffield for the added one night in the city and then he had three sell-out nights in Birmingham's NIA to play. Birmingham

was where he was due to finish his tour on the 23rd of that month and was his fifth time playing the tour at that venue, which holds over 12,000 people sitting and has hosted everything from the Eurovision Song Contest to WWF Rebellion matches to Beyoncé concerts. But due to the postponed shows, it would be a few more weeks before he was able to 'put the show in the can'.

'When I walk off stage on November 23,' he told the *Metro* several months earlier, 'it's over. That's it. The show is in the can, I've committed it to tape and then I go and write a brand new show.'

On Tuesday, 12 and Wednesday, 13 November he was in Liverpool at the Echo Arena, while on Thursday, 14 and Friday 15th, he played two dates at Nottingham's Capital FM Arena. That weekend was a bit of a breather as the following week would be a full-on barrage of DVD promotion – the DVD was out on Monday, 18 November and Micky would be appearing on *BBC Breakfast* and Alan Carr's *Chatty Man* show to get all the publicity he could.

BBC Breakfast presenters Bill Turnbull and Louise Minchin welcomed him to the sofa, which Micky had previously warned his fans about on Facebook.

'Just wanted to let you all know that my new DVD is out today,' he wrote. 'Which is just as well as I was up at 6.30 this morning plugging it on Breakfast TV.'

Bill and Louise were keen to talk about the DVD, which Micky admitted did make him nervous as his first tour and DVD had been such a hit.

'The Out Out tour was so successful that I knew I had my work cut out to write another DVD and another touring show. You can't just sit there.'

But perhaps the most exciting news to come out of the interview was the revelation that he was busy writing his own TV sitcom.

'I've been sitting down writing the first drafts of a sitcom which I want to do,' he told Bill. 'It's going to be purely based on me. I didn't want to expand beyond that. I know myself, write about what you know.'

'So it's about an East End boy who makes good and then eats organic food and stuff?' asked Bill.

'Yes, and then occasionally pops to KFC for a treat. Is it going to be called Micky? We might go a bit further than that but yeah, probably as simple as that. It's about my life now, living where I do in Dulwich. I don't want to be somebody else, I can only play myself.'

The plan was that there would be a trial episode filmed early in 2014, with Micky confirming that the TV bosses were 'looking to do the pilot in the New Year.' Bill asked how he found being a stand-up and the work involved and about life on tour. Micky replied: 'It's hard, you work every weekend when you're on the circuit, every weekend for 14 years. That's how you do it.

'There are glamorous moments to being on tour, but you get to a point where you understand why people smash hotel rooms up. Not that you'd ever do it but you get to the point where you're in your 15th different

hotel and you can't work out how to turn on the lights and there are tiny little things wrong with them... It all builds up.'

Micky couldn't resist the chance to present a bit off the show either, reading from the sofa on the autocue the plug about himself. He turned to the camera and said, 'Micky's DVD *Back in the Game* is out today and he's on tour around the country. He's a wonderful human being...' before Bill cut him off.

He was also on Absolute Radio with Christian O'Connell, talking about the DVD and his sitcom pilot.

'We've done about 100 shows so far this year, then we've got a few more to go, then have a nice break for Christmas before I start work on a pilot for a new sitcom. I can't tell you much about it, but it's early conversations about my life, all the trouble I get in living where I do now, living in a middle-class suburb but still essentially having a council estate mentality.'

With his show, *Was It Something I Said?*, still on air until 24 November and *I Love My Country* just finished, as well as all the DVD plugging, Micky commented to an interviewer that his mug was on every channel again at the moment. But there was one particular show he was desperate to return to, Sky1's *A League of Their Own*.

'How many panel shows am I doing at the moment? Four million. Not really, I'm doing *Was It Something I Said?* with David Mitchell, which we're probably doing a second series of. I'm hoping to get back on *A League*

of Their Own because I'm the Rolls-Royce of a man and that's where I belong.'

On 22 November he appeared on episode 13 of Series 11 of Alan Carr's *Chatty Man* show. He was a guest alongside Sheridan Smith and some of the cast from *Made in Chelsea* – Spencer Matthews, Mark-Francis Vandelli Orlov-Romanovsky, Binky Felstead, Lucy Watson and Andy Jordan. Alan introduced him as the luscious-locks stand-up and the pearly king of comedy and the pair shared a rather exaggerated hug when he came down the stairs.

'The cat's out the bag, Alan! We've been lovers for so many years, haven't we?' he jested.

Micky told Alan about his love of shoplifting and how he doesn't ever worry about getting caught – especially not now as he would be able to pay anyone off:

'The British people love a little tickle – the day we stop we become Americans! I have had to curb it a little bit but I wouldn't really care if I got caught thieving. I'd just pay the person off with the money I've got now. You can buy justice, history has taught us that the more money you've got, the less chance you've got of being banged up. Like politicians and bankers.' To which the audience started clapping.

Alan then told him that Micky's stand-up DVD always picked up audience footage of the crowd being in absolute hysterics while some comics have crowd reactions of them checking their watches.

'You're like a cockney Jesus to them!' he told Micky. 'Are cockneys becoming an endangered species?'

'I am going to start a charity for the pearly children,' Micky deadpanned. 'Cos what are they going to do with all the buttons? That's the question. No, I don't worry about the East Ender too much, they tend to look after themselves quite well.'

Carr then showed the same clip that *BBC Breakfast* had used of Micky's DVD, the sketch where he pretends he is his wife ending a phonecall – the 'bye, bye, bye…' gag.

Promoting the DVD helped. Within two weeks of it being released, Back in the Game was at No.1 in the stand-up charts (outselling *Mrs Brown's Boys* at No.2 and Miranda Hart, who was at No.3) and No.14 in the overall video charts, just below the *Despicable Me* twin-pack.

With only a few weeks left of the tour to go, Micky was back on stage on the 21st and 22nd in Manchester at the MEN Arena before hitting Birmingham NIA Arena for the last time. There was then just a week in between the official end of his tour and his rearranged dates, which he played at the O2. That was it. He was now able to put his feet up. Or maybe not quite yet…

Chapter 19

AND THE WINNER IS...

'If you're a funny person, and you go through life pointing out what's funny, then you're halfway there. The other half is boiling that down to its essence. I'm always so busy trying to make the moment work that I never actually step back and go, "Look what I've done, this is amazing." It's your mates who do that for you. If you're truly in the moment on stage, you can't also appreciate it as a spectator.'

entertainment.ie

Micky had appeared on *The One Show* at the beginning of 2013 and now he was back on the sofa with Alex Jones and Matt Baker as the year drew to a close. Seated in the Christmassy set of the show on 11 December, all festive cheer and thoughts of 'goodwill to all men' disappeared and he caused a little bit of controversy

when he upset one of the most famous scousers in the country, Cilla Black.

Alex was quizzing him about his DVD and asking him about his stories of dabbling in a bit of stealing, prompting Micky to point at the former *Blind Date* presenter.

'Cilla's from Liverpool, you know all about it too, dontcha? There's not an honest person in Liverpool. I've been to Liverpool, they don't stop! The scouser and the cockney are very similar in that respect,' he told her.

Cilla was shocked. She couldn't believe he was slating her hometown. 'They are lovely in Liverpool, you'll never be able to go there again!' she warned him.

'Of course I will, it's one of my favourite cities. They'll celebrate me there, probably give me a statue or something,' he retorted.

It was typical deadpan Micky and Alex and Matt weren't sure how to try and keep Cilla calm!

'Right, moving on...' gushed Matt, 'Micky's DVD is available now, not that many people in Liverpool will be buying it.'

'No, they'll be stealing it!' responded Micky.

The furore made for hilarious teatime viewing; social networking sites were tweeting about Micky's comments while websites as random as Mumsnet were also discussing the show. The comments on the Mumsnet forum were mainly in Micky's favour too.

'Did anyone just see Cilla Black's barely contained apoplectic rage at Micky Flanagan's comments about

Liverpool?' wrote one. 'Good for Micky Flanagan!' wrote another.

On Saturday, 14 December he appeared on ITV's quiz show, *The Chase*, as part of a celebrity special. Four well-known celebrities were appearing and had to work together to try and win thousands of pounds for charity. Former *Strictly Come Dancing* judge Arlene Phillips, garden designer Diarmuid Gavin, TV presenter Helen Skelton and Micky all took part in that episode and Micky was keen to let his fans know where they could donate:

'Just to say I'm on the *Chase* (my level of quiz) this Saturday at 7pm. It's in aid of Missing People and if you would like to donate to this amazing charity, here's the link.'

The Chase, hosted by Bradley Walsh, pits contestants against an opponent who represents 'the bank', known as 'the chaser'. A team of 4 contestants then try to amass as much money as possible for a team kitty by answering quick-fire questions in a 60-second round. That money is then put on a money board and each contestant has to get his money 'home' before the chaser catches up. Micky enjoyed the quiz game experience and even more so as it raised money for a good cause, but it was time to spend Christmas with his family, and make sure his dad had everyone around him in support.

He did find time to thank his Facebook fans for their continued support on 23 December and simply wrote, 'Just wanted to say have a great Christmas and New Year

and thank you for all your support. Here's to a great 2014, love Micky.'

Professionally, it was a good end to 2013. His tour had gone beyond all expectation and comedy website Chortle revealed that he topped the charts of comedians whose tickets were most sought-after that year. He was No.1 on the list of comedian searches on the Ticketmaster website, followed by Lee Evans and Mrs Brown's Boys.

'It's fantastic news he's the number 1 comic,' confirmed his agent Christian Knowles. 'We're delighted that Micky's talent and hard work has been rewarded.'

In January 2014 Micky's wish to return to *A League of Their Own* came true when filming started for the new series and he was asked to take part in a particularly amusing sporting event – an exhibition match at the ZEO International Netball Tri-series against an all-star line-up. Micky, James Corden, Freddie Flintoff, Jamie Redknapp, Jack Whitehall and Laura Whitmore all took part in the match at Wembley and dressed in fetching Union Jack red singlet vests. The match was England v England A, with Jamie playing Centre, Freddie Goal Defence and Micky Goal Keeper.

The year 2014 was all about new challenges and on 11 March it was announced that Micky, alongside Frankie Boyle, Stewart Lee and Bob Mortimer and others, would be recording his own show for the BBC website, iPlayer, which was getting a revamp after cost-cutting measures forced BBC3 off air to its new home of the iPlayer.

'Each comedian is doing a comedy short exclusively for BBC iPlayer, a "passion piece" they've always wanted to do,' revealed Victoria Jaye, head of TV content for iPlayer. Micky's was called 'Micky Flanagan's Foxageddon'.

At the end of February it was also announced that Micky was one of the celebrities involved in the annual Teenage Cancer Trust show held at the Royal Albert Hall from 24 to 30 March. The Who front man, Roger Daltrey, helmed the show with Noel Gallagher and the pair compiled a line-up that included The Cure, who gave two three-hour performances to mark the 35th anniversary of their debut album. Ed Sheeran kicked off the gigs while other headliners were Paolo Nutini and OneRepublic. One night was devoted to comedy and on Tuesday, 25 March, Micky, alongside Jason Manford, John Bishop and Patrick Kielty all took to the stage to entertain the fans – 35,000 people packed the venue over the 7 nights and all the proceeds from the show went towards providing specialist care and support for young people with cancer. Jason, who hosted the evening, also welcomed newcomers like Rob Beckett and Hal Cruttenden to the stage and the evening was a great success.

Micky had also been nominated in the 2014 Chortle Comedy Awards too, which *Time Out* magazine described as 'gongs that are practically the Oscars for jobbing circuit comedians.' Run by the internet comedy bible, Chortle, fans could vote for who they wanted to win in each category, with Micky nominated in the Best

tour category for Back in the Game, alongside Barry Humphries: Dame Edna's Farewell Tour, Bo Burham: What and Harry Hill: Sausage Time. Micky was delighted to scoop the prize for his second tour, especially as it was voted for by the public.

So, what next for Micky? What does the future hold for the stand-up/entertainer/sitcom-to-be star? In an interview with the *Metro* he revealed one of his unfulfilled career ambitions was to make a film about life in London in the decade he grew up in, and elaborated to entertainment.ie:

'I want to make a film about London in the late 1970s and early 1980s – to capture that turning point when it went from being what I consider to be post-war London to what we see now as a slightly fractured city, where money seems to be king and the way of life and communities have broken down.'

While his notion of making a film about London is still an ambition, it was announced in May 2014 that he would be filming a new travel documentary show for Sky1, with his best pal, Noel Lynch. This new 4-part series was slated to see the duo hit the road and cycle around France, visiting some of the most iconic landmarks along the way, including the Eiffel Tower, the vineyards of Champagne and World War One cemeteries. The show was described as 'the ultimate test of man's endurance', and each hour-long episode would chart Micky and Noel's progress around the country as they cycled their very own 'fantasy Tour de France'.

'Life is a journey, and I like journeys, even French ones,' Micky revealed at a Sky1 press event when the series was announced. 'This will be a journey of physical and mental obstacles and I will overcome them all... once I have bought the bike!'

It seems poignant to finish this book by looking back at the footage of Micky and his mum at her house in Bethnal Green, which features on his Out Out DVD as an 'extra'. She asks him about his future and tells Micky, after apologising for being maudlin, that she knows for a lot of comedians, their biggest regret is that their parents didn't see their success or were alive to see how popular they had become.

'That has been really nice, it has, that we've seen this. High five, Mick!'

'Thanks, Mum.'

'Where do you see yourself in 10 years' time, though, son? You've got a nice house, a nice wife, a lovely son... What's next?'

'A bigger house! No, no... I still want to be enjoying it. And if people are still coming and they're still laughing and still enjoying it and I'm still enjoying it, then we'll carry on. Am I ever scared it will all stop? Of course. But that's why you've got to enjoy it and not worry too much. And I've still got my window cleaning bucket and my pearly paintbrushes in the basement if it all goes tits up...'